THIS BOOK STINKS!

**GROSS GARBAGE,
ROTTEN RUBBISH,
and the SCIENCE OF TRASH**

SARAH WASSNER FLYNN

NATIONAL GEOGRAPHIC
WASHINGTON, D.C.

CONTENTS

CHAPTER 1:
The Bin and Beyond

CHAPTER 2:
Trashing the Earth

CHAPTER 3:
All About
Recycling

CHAPTER 4:
Food (Waste) for Thought

CHAPTER 5:
Dirty Work

CHAPTER 6:
The Future
of Garbage

CHAPTER 7:
Take Out the Trash

It's stinky. It's icky. And it's absolutely everywhere. Yep, we're talking trash—and everything about it. Sure, the filthy stuff may get a bad rap, but not everything about garbage is gross. In fact, a lot that has to do with trash is totally cool. And that's not a bunch of rubbish!

Flip through these pages to fill up on fascinating facts about the filthy stuff, from how much of it is piling up on our planet and contributing to climate change to the cool things artists and innovators are producing out of junk. Read all about recycling, get the lowdown on landfills, and find out why some people choose to eat old food (yes, really!). Discover the art of Dumpster diving, get the inside scoop on one of the world's most dangerous careers, and explore cool new inventions that will change the way we'll handle waste in the future.

These stinky stories and stats aren't just fun to read about. They can also be used as tools to help you make smarter choices about the amount of trash you toss every day. From wiser ways to get rid of your rubbish to fun ideas for upcycling, or reusing, your old stuff, you'll be able to play a part in making the world a much less wasteful place.

CHAPTER 1

THE BIN AND BEYOND

WE THROW A LOT AWAY. HOW MUCH, EXACTLY? EXPERTS ESTIMATE THAT AROUND THE WORLD, THE AVERAGE PERSON TOSSES 2.6 POUNDS (1.2 KG) OF TRASH EVERY SINGLE DAY. THE UNITED STATES ALONE GENERATES ABOUT 254 MILLION TONS (230 MILLION MT) PER YEAR. AND THE AMOUNT OF GARBAGE WILL ONLY GROW IN THE COMING YEARS—EXPERTS SAY THAT BY 2025, THE WORLD WILL GENERATE NEARLY 2 BILLION TONS (1.8 BILLION MT) ANNUALLY. SO WHAT'S IN YOUR GARBAGE—AND WHERE DOES IT ALL GO? HERE, WE EXPLORE THE VARIOUS TYPES OF TRASH, PLUS THE WAYS WE GET RID OF RUBBISH.

IT WAS LIKE THIS WHEN I FOUND IT ...

ALL TYPES OF TRASH

WHEN YOU THINK OF WHAT'S IN YOUR GARBAGE CAN, THE FIRST THING THAT JUMPS TO YOUR MIND MAY BE THAT BROWN APPLE CORE YOU FOUND AT THE BOTTOM OF YOUR BACKPACK OR LAST NIGHT'S LEFTOVERS. BUT TRASH DOESN'T CONSIST ONLY OF COFFEE GROUNDS AND STINKY BANANA PEELS. IN FACT, FOOD WASTE REPRESENTS JUST A SMALL PERCENTAGE OF YOUR HOUSEHOLD WASTE. THE REST OF IT COMES FROM STUFF WITH FAR LESS OF AN ICK FACTOR.

IN THE U.S. ALONE, NEARLY TWO MILLION TONS (1.8 MILLION MT) OF TRASH ENDS UP IN LANDFILLS EVERY YEAR.

OLD ELECTRONICS—ALSO KNOWN AS E-WASTE—MAKE UP THE WORLD'S FASTEST-GROWING SOURCE OF WASTE.

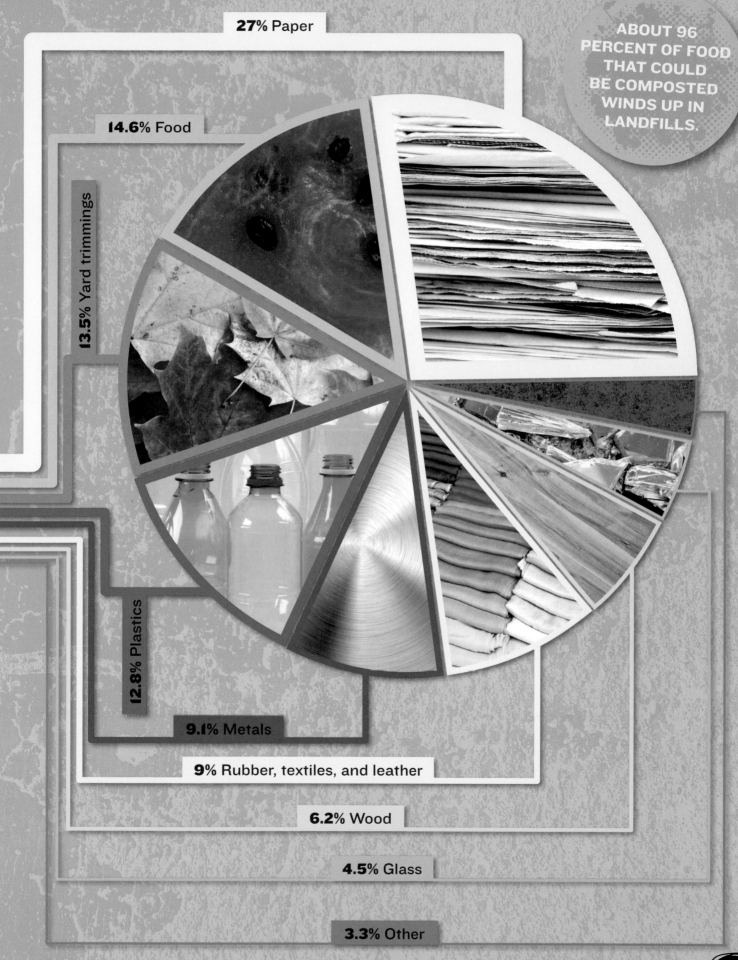

27% Paper

14.6% Food

13.5% Yard trimmings

12.8% Plastics

9.1% Metals

9% Rubber, textiles, and leather

6.2% Wood

4.5% Glass

3.3% Other

ABOUT 96 PERCENT OF FOOD THAT COULD BE COMPOSTED WINDS UP IN LANDFILLS.

*STATISTICS ONLY APPLICABLE TO THE UNITED STATES

AROUND THE WORLD, PEOPLE THROW AWAY ROUGHLY FOUR MILLION TONS OF TRASH [3.6 MILLION MT] EVERY DAY.

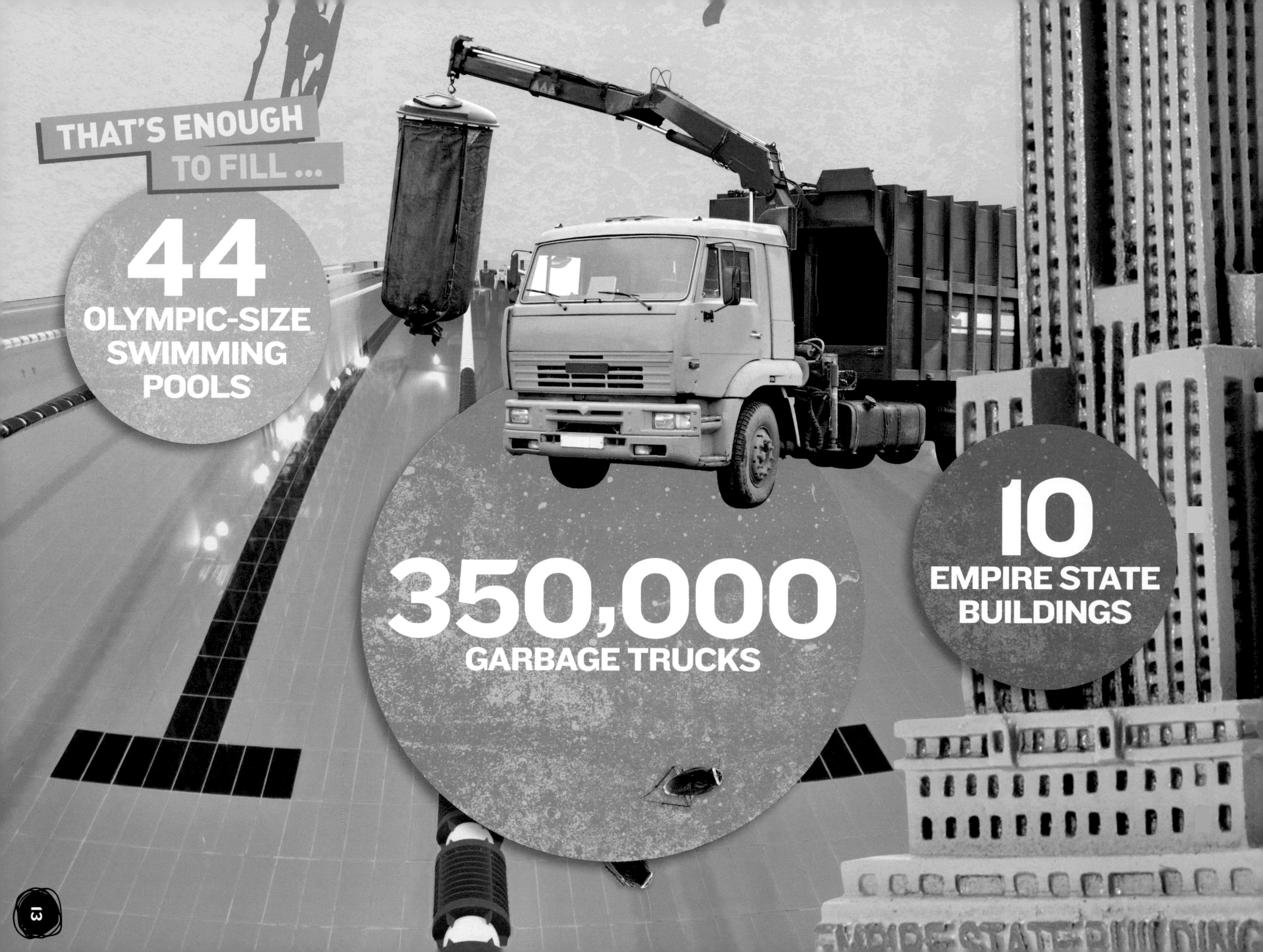

THAT'S ENOUGH TO FILL ...

44
OLYMPIC-SIZE
SWIMMING
POOLS

350,000
GARBAGE TRUCKS

10
EMPIRE STATE
BUILDINGS

13

WHERE OUR TRASH WINDS UP

IT'S LIKELY THAT THE LAST TIME YOU SEE YOUR TRASH IS WHEN IT GETS HAULED INTO THE GARBAGE TRUCK IN FRONT OF YOUR HOUSE. BUT WHERE DOES IT GO FROM THERE?

These numbers are based on trash generated in the UNITED STATES only.

RECYCLED or COMPOSTED: 27%

27 percent of trash, including glass, paper, and some plastic, is **broken down** into material to create new items, while grass clippings, branches, and food waste can be turned into **yard fertilizer**.

BURIED: 57%

57 percent of our trash goes to **landfills,** large areas set aside for storing trash.

BURNED: 16%

16 percent of trash is sent to **incinerators** to be combusted.

LANDFILL AND DUMP: WHAT'S THE DIFFERENCE?

The words "landfill" and "dump" may be used interchangeably, but there is a distinction between the two. While both are large areas designated for trash, a landfill is technically a carefully designed structure that follows strict environmental regulations. Around the world, rules vary from place to place, but in the United States and some other developed nations, landfills are highly engineered to avoid polluting the environment. A dump does not necessarily have the same standards. A dump is typically just a hole in the ground into which trash is piled.

LANDFILL LOWDOWN

IN THE UNITED STATES ALONE, THERE ARE CLOSE TO 2,000 LANDFILLS, WHICH ARE A FINAL RESTING SPOT FOR NEARLY HALF THE TRASH PRODUCED IN THE COUNTRY. HERE'S HOW LANDFILLS WORK.

LEACHATE COLLECTION

a high-tech **wastewater system** used to collect and treat **leachates,** the brew of noxious chemicals oozing from the trash

STORM WATER DRAINAGE

usually a system of **plastic drainage pipes** that collect rainwater dripping through the landfill to **prevent contamination**

BOTTOM LINER

a layered system, usually made of **clay, sand,** or **plastic,** designed to keep buried waste from coming in contact with soil and groundwater

CAP

a covering of about 18 inches (46 cm) of **clay, a plastic liner,** and roughly two feet (61 cm) of **soil** used to **seal in the waste, eliminate odor,** and **prevent pests** like mice and birds from picking at the trash

METHANE COLLECTION

a series of **pipes for collecting and venting methane** (a dangerous greenhouse gas created during the decomposition of garbage) so that it can be **converted into energy** used to fuel power plants, cars, homes, and more

CELL

an **isolated area** in a landfill where a certain amount of waste is dumped and either **compacted or crushed**

WASTE LANDS

What happens when a LANDFILL ... well, FILLS WITH TRASH? More than likely, it'll get a MAKEOVER—and may even turn into a place for you TO PLAY.

DON'T JUST DUMP IT!

Warning! Think twice before you toss these items into your trash can. Considered household hazardous waste (HHW), they have the potential to harm sanitation workers or contaminate the surrounding environment. So if you need to get rid of any of these potentially dangerous materials, take them to your local waste facility to find out where to properly pitch them.

BATTERIES

FLUORESCENT BULBS

OIL-BASED PAINTS

MOTOR OIL

NAIL POLISH REMOVER

BLEACH

Mount Hiriya, a popular peak in Israel, was once a dumping ground but has since gone green.

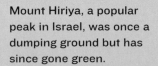

THE TRUTH BEHIND THE TRASH

Popular spot Mount Trashmore in Virginia, U.S.A., may appear to be a lush, green park with a sizable hill at its center. But buried deep within that grassy mound are tons of trash. At 60 feet (18 m) tall and 800 feet (244 m) long, this iconic peak was created by compacting layers of solid waste and clean soil. Former landfills around the world have followed suit, like 197-foot (60-m)-tall Mount Hiriya near Tel Aviv, Israel, while others are used for wildlife reserves or parks and athletic fields, like Freshkills Park in New York City. So the next time you hit a new green space in your neighborhood, there just may be some stinky stuff lurking beneath your feet!

THERE ARE TWO MOUNTAINS MADE OUT OF TRASH IN VIRGINIA BEACH, VIRGINIA, U.S.A.

A PRO SOCCER TEAM IN DALLAS, TEXAS, U.S.A., PLAYS ON A FIELD BUILT ON TOP OF AN OLD LANDFILL.

6 THINGS YOU DIDN'T KNOW ABOUT E-WASTE

THE AMOUNT OF **E-WASTE** PRODUCED **AROUND THE WORLD** WOULD FILL **1.15 MILLION 18-WHEELER TRUCKS.**

IN THE U.S., ONLY ABOUT **40 PERCENT** OF **DISCARDED ELECTRONICS** ARE **RECYCLED** OR **REUSED.**

WHERE DOES THE STUFF YOU CAN'T STASH IN YOUR TRASH CAN GO? BIG APPLIANCES LIKE MICROWAVES, VACUUMS, WASHING MACHINES—PLUS ELECTRONICS LIKE SMARTPHONES AND COMPUTERS—ARE ALL CONSIDERED ELECTRONIC WASTE, OR "E-WASTE," AND SOME 50 MILLION TONS (45 MILLION MT) OF IT IS TOSSED EACH YEAR.

EVERY YEAR, THE **AVERAGE PERSON** IN THE UNITED STATES **PRODUCES 66 POUNDS** (30 KG) OF E-WASTE—ROUGHLY **THE SAME WEIGHT** AS A

10-YEAR-OLD.

TOGETHER, THE **UNITED STATES** AND **CHINA** PRODUCE JUST OVER **A THIRD** OF THE **WORLD'S** E-WASTE.

THE E-WASTE TOTAL IS **EXPECTED TO RISE** TO **55 MILLION TONS** (50 MILLION MT) BY **2018.**

RECYCLING **A MILLION** CELL PHONES CAN RECOVER ABOUT **50 POUNDS** (23 KG) OF **GOLD.**

TRASH TIMELINE

WHAT TAKES THE LONGEST TO BREAK DOWN?

APPLE CORE: **TWO MONTHS**

PLASTIC SHOPPING BAG: **20 YEARS**

BANANA PEEL: **A FEW WEEKS**

*TIME ESTIMATES ARE SUBJECT TO CONDITIONS. IN THIS CASE, WE ARE ASSUMING ITEMS ARE EXPOSED TO WATER, SUNLIGHT, AND AIR.

DISPOSABLE DIAPER: **450 YEARS**

GLASS BOTTLES: **1,000,000 YEARS**

PRINTER INK CARTRIDGE: **1,000 YEARS**

CHAPTER 2

TRASHING THE EARTH

WASTE IS A WORLDWIDE PROBLEM. AND THE EFFECTS OF HAVING SO MUCH OF THE SMELLY STUFF PILING UP AROUND THE GLOBE ARE BEING FELT EVERYWHERE. NOT ONLY IS THERE TRASH SCATTERED IN OUR SEAS AND EVEN FLOATING IN SPACE, BUT GARBAGE HAS A DIRECT IMPACT ON THE ENVIRONMENT. DECOMPOSING TRASH IS DIRECTLY LINKED TO THE PRODUCTION OF HARMFUL GREENHOUSE GASES. IN FACT, THE ENVIRONMENTAL PROTECTION AGENCY (EPA) ESTIMATES THAT LANDFILLS ARE THE THIRD LEADING CAUSE OF METHANE EMISSIONS IN THE U.S. ALONE. SO JUST BY SIMPLY SITTING AROUND IN LANDFILLS AND DUMPS, GARBAGE IS CAUSING CLIMATE CHANGE.

THE GOOD NEWS? THERE'S PLENTY THAT WE CAN ALL DO TO STALL THESE SCARY STATS, LIKE RECYCLING. HERE'S MORE ABOUT HOW TRASH IS AFFECTING THE ENTIRE PLANET—AND BEYOND.

WORLD'S MOST WASTEFUL

TOO MUCH TRASH ISN'T JUST A PROBLEM FOR THE UNITED STATES. TAKE A LOOK AT HOW OTHER COUNTRIES' ANNUAL WASTE TOTALS WEIGH IN.

FRANCE

99,751 tons
(90,493 MT)

UNITED KINGDOM

107,391 tons
(97,423 MT)

RUSSIA

110,261 tons
(100,027 MT)

INDIA

120,801 tons
(109,589 MT)

GERMANY

140,893 tons
(127,816 MT)

KEY

= 50,000 TONS (45,000 MT) PER DAY

JAPAN

159,247 tons
(144,466 MT)

BRAZIL

164,350 tons
(149,096 MT)

CHINA

573,806 tons
(520,548 MT)

UNITED STATES

688,614 tons
(624,700 MT)

What: Trutier
Where: Port-au-Prince, Haiti
Size: .36 square mile (0.9 sq km)
Filthy Fact: One organization is using compost produced at Trutier to grow mango trees.

What: Cidade Estrutural
Where: Brasília, Brazil
Size: .53 square mile (1.4 sq km)
Filthy Fact: Receiving 18,000 pounds (8,165 kg) of trash per day, it is the largest dump in Latin America.

What: Bantar Gebang
Where: Jakarta, Indonesia
Size: .43 square mile (1.1 sq km)
Filthy Fact: This giant mound of rotting rubbish is known locally as "the Mountain."

What: Apex Landfill
Where: Las Vegas, Nevada, U.S.A.
Size: 3.4 square miles (8.9 sq km)
Filthy Fact: Up to 20 trucks dump some 600 tons (544 MT) of garbage in this landfill every hour.

SUPER DUMPS!

THAT'S A LOT OF TRASH! DIG INTO THE BIGGEST DUMPS AND LANDFILLS AROUND THE WORLD.

What: Rumpke Sanitary Landfill
Where: Colerain Township, Ohio, U.S.A.
Size: .78 square mile (2 sq km)
Filthy Fact: Lightning once hit "Mount Rumpke" and caused a landslide that exposed buried waste covering an area as wide as 15 soccer fields.

POWERED BY TRASH

PURIFIED GAS collected from landfills in the United States can create enough **ENERGY** to power and heat nearly **TWO MILLION** homes.

THE TRUTH BEHIND THE TRASH

One of the most heated issues when it comes to getting rid of trash? Whether it's better to bury it or burn it. Both have been bashed for hurting the environment: Incinerating trash pumps heat, toxic ash, and gases into the atmosphere, while waste decomposing in landfills produces methane, a superpotent greenhouse gas that erodes the ozone layer and plays a part in climate change.

This sounds scary, but the news isn't so grim. There are ways to create clean energy using both options. Many landfills have built-in pipes to capture and purify the methane so that it can be used in a positive way, such as providing electricity to homes and schools. And at waste-to-energy (WTE) incinerators, the heat energy from the fire turns turbines to produce clean energy. Because large incinerators can combust some 3,000 tons (2,722 MT) of material (including household garbage, wood, tires, and scrap metal) per day, they have the ability to produce an abundance of energy. In fact, one major incinerator in Baltimore, Maryland, U.S.A., produces enough electricity to help run the city's Inner Harbor as well as its football and baseball stadiums. Now that's a *bright* idea!

ABOUT 175,000 TONS (158,757 MT) OF TRASH CAN PRODUCE ENOUGH ENERGY TO POWER SOME 15,000 HOMES PER YEAR.

SHENZHEN, CHINA, IS BUILDING THE WORLD'S LARGEST WASTE-TO-ENERGY PLANT, CAPABLE OF BURNING MORE THAN 5,500 TONS (5,000 MT) OF TRASH EVERY DAY.

FLOATING FILTH

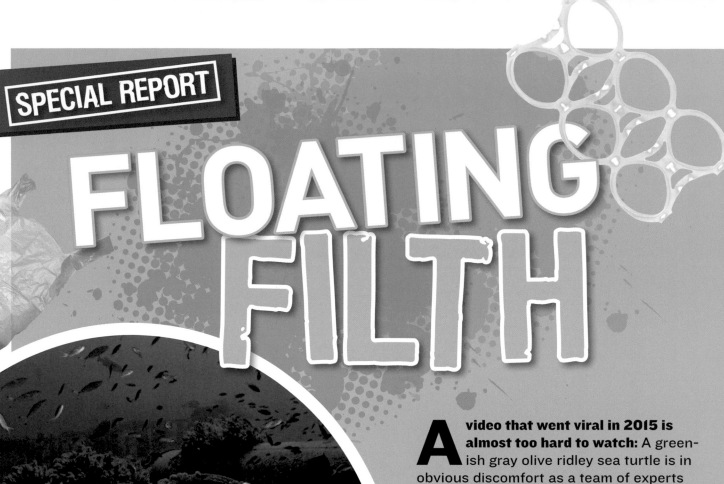

A video that went viral in 2015 is almost too hard to watch: A greenish gray olive ridley sea turtle is in obvious discomfort as a team of experts work to dislodge something deep within its nostril. At first, they think it's a worm. But after wrenching the item out with pliers, the experts are stunned to see what it really is: a plastic drinking straw.

Sadly, it's not uncommon to find marine animals that are entangled in plastic or other types of trash floating in the ocean. According to one study that looked at the world's 192 coastal countries, 8.8 million tons (8 million MT) of plastic pollution made its way into the ocean every year. Across the Earth's oceans, there are five gyres—massive, slow-rotating whirlpools caused by currents—that suck up trash. In the North Pacific between Hawaii and California, some scientists estimate that a giant, swirling mass of trash—known as the Great Pacific Garbage Patch—could be twice the size of Texas. And that's just the tip of the trashberg.

The impact of this floating filth goes much deeper than just the surface level.

Left: A sea turtle gracefully glides over a sunken ship in the Red Sea.
Right: A bottlenose dolphin nibbles on a not-so-nutritious snack: the plastic rings of a six-pack drink holder.

Some of the trash sinks to the bottom of the ocean, and some is heavy enough to lurk just under the surface. Aside from animals mistaking pieces of plastic for food or becoming tangled in trash, the pollution also has a devastating impact on life in the sea. Millions of tiny pieces of plastic accumulate in the water and block the sunlight—similar to smog in the sky—directly impacting small marine organisms known as autotrophs that feed off the sun's rays. Because autotrophs are at the bottom of the food chain, a lack of sustenance for them means the entire ocean's ecosystem can be thrown out of whack.

So what can be done about this? Experts say it all starts with reducing the amount of plastic we use across the planet. Opting for reusable containers or those made with marine biodegradable components is a better option. It's a small step, but a step in the right direction when it comes to protecting our oceans and the animals in them.

MICROBEADS: A BIG ISSUE

They're tiny plastic beads found in household items like face wash and toothpaste. But they're causing a huge problem in our oceans. No bigger than a pencil point, microbeads go down the drain in your home, slip through the filters in the water system, and eventually make their way into rivers, streams, and ultimately oceans at a rate of eight trillion a day in the United States. Because these toxic beads look a lot like fish food, it's not uncommon for bigger fish and sea turtles to munch on them—a dish that could be deadly.

Ocean conservationists are working to ban microbeads from everyday products. And so far, it's working: The beads are now outlawed in the United States, the United Kingdom, and other countries with the hopes that these beads will soon be banished for good around the world.

Dutch inventor Boyan Slat came up with his ambitious plan to rid the world's oceans of plastic when he was just a teen.

A BRIGHT IDEA

No doubt, ocean waste is a huge problem, but 22-year-old Boyan Slat may have the solution. This Dutch inventor, who is the founder of the conservation group the Ocean Cleanup, is working on a 62-mile (100-km)-long floating barrier that uses the ocean's currents to filter and trap trash about 10 feet (3 m) below the water's surface. All told, it'll be the longest floating structure ever deployed in the ocean. And Boyan is hopeful it'll make a big impact, possibly removing more than 40 percent of the Great Pacific Garbage Patch within 10 years.

SWIMMING IN IT

A BY-THE-NUMBERS LOOK AT HOW MARINE ANIMALS ARE IMPACTED BY OCEAN TRASH

700 SPECIES OF ANIMALS ARE SEVERELY THREATENED BECAUSE OF OCEAN WASTE.

22 MILLION TONS (20 MILLION MT) OF CARBON DIOXIDE IS ABSORBED BY THE OCEAN EACH DAY BECAUSE OF TRASH.

443 ANIMALS AND BIRDS WERE FOUND TRAPPED BY MARINE DEBRIS DURING A RECENT INTERNATIONAL COASTAL CLEANUP.

10% OF ALL DEAD ANIMALS FOUND IN BEACH CLEANUPS WORLDWIDE WERE ENTANGLED IN PLASTIC BAGS.

90% OF SEABIRDS EAT PLASTIC TRASH.

20% OF FISH FOUND DURING ONE EXPEDITION HAD PLASTIC IN THEIR STOMACHS.

52% OF SEA TURTLES WORLDWIDE HAVE ACCIDENTALLY EATEN PLASTIC TRASH IN THE OCEAN.

5 TRILLION PIECES OF PLASTIC (NOT INCLUDING MICROBEADS) ARE FLOATING IN THE WORLD'S SEAS.

9 THINGS YOU DIDN'T KNOW ABOUT WASTE IN SPACE

A GLOVE DROPPED DURING THE FIRST AMERICAN SPACEWALK **IN 1965** IS STILL **ORBITING THE EARTH.**

AN AVERAGE OF ONE PIECE OF **DEBRIS** FELL TO EARTH **EACH DAY** DURING THE LAST **FIVE DECADES.**

OF THE MILLIONS OF PIECES OF **SPACE DEBRIS,** MORE THAN **21,000 OBJECTS** ARE LARGER THAN A **SOFTBALL.**

ALL THE **SPACE JUNK** FLOATING AROUND WEIGHS ABOUT **14 MILLION POUNDS** (6.4 MILLION KG)— MATCHING THE WEIGHT OF ABOUT **1,000 AFRICAN ELEPHANTS!**

EVER WONDER WHAT HAPPENS WHEN A SATELLITE BREAKS APART OR A PIECE OF EQUIPMENT SPLINTERS OFF A SPACECRAFT? THIS MATERIAL IS CALLED SPACE DEBRIS, OR SPACE JUNK, AND EXPERTS SAY THERE'S A MASSIVE AMOUNT OF IT ORBITING EARTH. TRAVELING AT BREAKNECK SPEEDS, SPACE JUNK PRESENTS A DANGEROUS THREAT TO THE INTERNATIONAL SPACE STATION, SPACE SHUTTLES—AND THE FUTURE OF SPACE EXPLORATION.

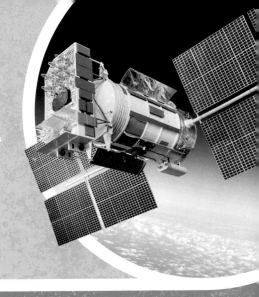

SPACE TRASH MAY ZIP AROUND AT UP TO **18,000 MILES AN HOUR** (28,968 KM/H), WHICH IS **AS FAST AS A ROCKET!**

SATELLITES AND **SPACE DEBRIS** COME WITHIN **FIVE MILES** (8 KM) OF EACH OTHER ABOUT **1,000 TIMES A DAY.**

SPACE DEBRIS CAN STAY IN **ORBIT** FOR MORE THAN **100 YEARS.**

A CHUNK OF JUNK THE LENGTH OF A SOFA— **A FRAGMENT** OF AN **OLD ROCKET** —RECENTLY **ENTERED** THE EARTH'S ATMOSPHERE AND **SPLASH-LANDED** IN THE INDIAN OCEAN **NEAR SRI LANKA.**

THE **INTERNATIONAL SPACE STATION** HAS TO CHANGE ITS COURSE ABOUT **ONCE A YEAR** TO AVOID CONTACT WITH **LARGE PIECES OF DEBRIS.**

HOW WASTEFUL ARE YOU?

TAKE THIS QUIZ TO FIND OUT IF YOU ARE WINNING THE WASTE GAME. (PS: DON'T WORRY IF THE RESULTS DON'T MATCH YOUR PERSONALITY. IT'S JUST FOR FUN!)

1 You just ate the last of the chocolate-chip ice cream in your freezer. What do you do with the container?

A. Toss it in the trash can.

B. Toss it in the recycling bin.

C. Rinse it out and stash it away for a future art project.

2 A park in your neighborhood is covered with litter. How will you help?

A. Spend a couple hours with your family filling up a bunch of trash bags.

B. Pick up all the trash, then take all of the cans, newspapers, and plastic to your nearby recycling center.

C. Organize monthly cleanups and contact your local government about what can be done to prevent the litter issue.

3 Oops! You just spilled your juice all over the kitchen floor. What do you reach for to clean it up?

A. A bunch of napkins.

B. A few sheets of paper towels—the kind made out of recycled materials, of course.

C. A reusable rag that you can toss in the washing machine once you're through.

4 Yuck. A couple of your bananas have gone brown. What do you do with them?

A. Throw them away. Nothing's worse than mushy fruit.

B. Cut out the brown parts and eat what you can.

C. Throw them in a smoothie and add the peels to your compost bin.

5 It's the end of the school year and your backpack is filled with old worksheets. What will you do with them?

A. Dump the entire contents of your backpack into the trash.

B. Toss the paper into the recycling bin.

C. Go through each sheet and pull out whatever you can use for scrap paper; recycle the rest.

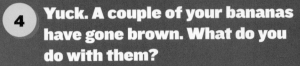

NOW TALLY UP YOUR ANSWERS AND FIND OUT WHAT KIND OF WASTER YOU ARE!

MOSTLY A's:
A WEE BIT WASTEFUL

You're tops when it comes to cleaning up, but when it comes to the amount of waste you toss, there's always more you can do. You have the power to do something—so look for little ways to make a difference. Whether it's convincing your family to switch over to reusable items around the house (like tote bags instead of plastic bags) or trying to find different ways to repurpose old things, you can be more mindful about the stuff you send to the bin.

MOSTLY B's:
RECYCLING ROCK STAR

You love the Earth and want to do everything you can to protect our planet. And that includes being super-aware of what can be recycled in your world. Cheers to you for being so green-minded! There's no doubt you'll lead by example, and soon your friends and family will become just as focused on recycling as you are.

MOSTLY C's:
LOW-WASTE WARRIOR

What other people may consider trash is truly your treasure—and that's an amazing thing! You have a talent for repurposing or "upcycling" old things and finding ways to breathe new life into what others may quickly toss away. So keep it up, the Earth thanks you!

CHAPTER 3

ALL ABOUT RECYCLING

TALK ABOUT A RECYCLING REVOLUTION! LESS THAN 40 YEARS AGO, HARDLY ANYONE HAD EVEN HEARD THE WORD "RECYCLING." TODAY IN THE UNITED STATES, WE REPURPOSE ABOUT 34 PERCENT OF OUR TRASH THROUGH THIS PROCESS. RECYCLING IS A PROVEN METHOD OF REDUCING WASTE AND HELPING OUR ENVIRONMENT. HERE'S MORE ABOUT THIS SMART WAY TO ELIMINATE WASTE—AND THE WILD WAYS PEOPLE AROUND THE WORLD ARE RETHINKING RECYCLING.

FROM RUBBISH TO RECYCLED

YOU SEPARATE YOUR PAPER FROM YOUR PLASTIC, RINSE OUT YOUR GLASS BOTTLES AND YOUR MILK JUGS—AND THEN WHAT? HERE'S A LOOK AT WHAT HAPPENS TO YOUR RECYCLABLES AFTER THEY'VE LEFT YOUR HOUSE.

SORT

Once your recyclables hit the recycling center, they're loaded on a **conveyor belt to be sorted.** First, plastic, paper, and metal are separated from one another, and then these categories are further separated into different types of items, like milk jugs and plastic water bottles.

SELL

Recycling plants then **sell** and **ship** the sorted bales to companies around the world to be used as material to **make new things.**

CRUSH

Big machines **squash** the sorted stuff into **giant cubes,** or bales. These cubes are so heavy that **forklifts** are required to move them around.

BREAK IT DOWN

So how does your trash become material to make new products? It all depends on the type of trash. Aluminum cans, for example, are melted down and then remolded into new cans, or used to make anything from airplane parts to bikes. Plastic bottles are broken down into tiny pieces, called "chips," which are then heated and melted into a thick liquid that's turned into a wool-like yarn used to create clothes or insulation or sleeping bags or winter coats. Glass is crushed and melted and then molded into new products such as bottles and jars. Paper is washed with soapy water—to remove things like inks, plastic film, staples, and glue—and then mixed with water, spread into large, thin sheets, and left to dry. The final product? More paper!

43

City: Los Angeles, California, U.S.A.
Recycling Rate: 76.4 percent
All-Star Stat: Over a six-year span, L.A. dropped its daily trash rate by more than 1.5 pounds (0.7 kg) per resident.

City: Neustadt an der Weinstraße, Germany
Recycling Rate: 70 percent
All-Star Stat: This small town recycles almost anything— and even has collection points for dead animals.

City: San Francisco, California, U.S.A.
Recycling Rate: 80 percent
All-Star Stat: San Francisco was the first U.S. city to ban plastic bags from its stores.

City: Vancouver, Canada
Recycling Rate: 60 percent
All-Star Stat: Vancouver-area residents can face fines for failing to recycle and compost.

City: Manshiyat Naser, Egypt
Recycling Rate: 90 percent
All-Star Stat: The people in this town—known as "Garbage City"—collect some 7,000 tons (6,350 MT) of garbage a day from Cairo and then sell the plastic bottles, paper, glass, and aluminum cans to factories.

RECYCLING STARS!

WHEN IT COMES TO THEIR RECYCLING RATES, THESE CITIES ARE LEADING THE CHARGE.

City: Kamikatsu, Japan
Recycling Rate: 80 percent
All-Star Stat: The town has 34 different categories for its recyclables, ranging from razors to pens.

City: Portland, Oregon, U.S.A.
Recycling Rate: 70 percent
All-Star Stat: People in Portland get their trash picked up only twice a month, but recyclables and food scraps are collected weekly.

A GLOBAL RACE TO ZERO WASTE

It's an ambitious goal, but one that some countries hope to achieve in less than 10 years. The aim? Zero waste, meaning every single piece of trash will be reused, recycled, or composted. The idea may seem impossible, but several spots are coming close.

Take Sweden, for example. Less than one percent of the country's household garbage ends up in landfills. Rather, the Swedes recycle nearly everything—some 1.5 billion bottles and cans annually—and the rest winds up at waste-to-energy plants to produce electricity. The program is so successful that Sweden actually imports trash from other places, such as the United Kingdom, Norway, and Ireland, to keep up the rapid pace of its incinerators.

Both Sweden **(above)** and Singapore **(right)** are worldwide leaders in recycling and waste reduction.

Other places narrowing in on zero waste? The Himalayan country of Bhutan is shooting for that status by 2030, while Singapore and Dubai have announced similar timelines. In the United States, individual cities like San Francisco and New York have also declared their dedication to going zero waste. The U.S. national park system, as well as major corporations like Lego and Nike, are also making big moves toward creating zero waste—all in an effort to make this world a cleaner place.

So what's the secret to zero waste? It's all about enforcing the rules of reducing, reusing, and recycling. In Sweden, for example, recycling stations must be no more than 984 feet (300 m) from any residential area. And in Bhutan—which is aspiring to become the world's first nation to have an all-organic farming system—composting from food scraps is the norm. Simple practices like this, as well as educating the public on the problems stemming from too much trash, can lead to major changes. And, perhaps, zero waste around the world one day.

Dubai—home to the famous Palm Jumeirah Island—is aiming to go waste-free by 2030.

CURBING
CLIMATE CHANGE

It was a meeting of the masterminds. For two weeks in 2015, world leaders from some 200 countries gathered together to focus on one important issue: climate change. In an effort to proactively address global warming, the leaders signed the Paris Agreement, a pact to cut down on pollution. In the pact, the countries pledged to limit the amount of greenhouse gases emitted by human activity, which includes reducing the rates of garbage rotting away in landfills. While the agreement may take some time to go into effect, it's a powerful move to protect the planet.

FROM FILTH TO FASHION

HOW SOME TRASH TRAVELS FROM THE RECYCLING CENTER TO THE RUNWAYS—AND EVEN TO YOUR CLOSET.

THREE DARING DRESSES

A **dress made from newspapers** and other found stuff, such as **bottle caps** and **gift-wrap ribbons**, is sure to make headlines.

It's a wrap! This frilly **frock is made** entirely out **of discarded candy wrappers.** Sweet!

One thing you can do with your family's stash of **old CDs?** Wear them!

FOUR AWESOME ACCESSORIES

A **hat** made out of an **old soccer ball** brings new meaning to the term **"header."**

This **eco-friendly bag** is made from **365 recycled computer keyboard keys.**

This **headpiece,** made from **recycled corrugated cardboard,** is hard to top!

This **bow tie** made out of an **old aluminum can** is both fashion-forward and **eco-friendly.**

LEVI STRAUSS & CO. MAKES JEANS OUT OF OLD COTTON T-SHIRTS.

AN ARTIST IN NEW ORLEANS, LOUISIANA, U.S.A., CREATES MOSAICS OUT OF MARDI GRAS BEADS AND OTHER TRASH FOUND THROUGHOUT THE CITY.

Order up! One creative company called Garbage Gone Glam made this dress out of diner menus. Other things they've made? A cocktail dress out of playing cards and a ball gown out of old magazines!

THIS TO THAT

TOTAL TRANSFORMATIONS OF RECYCLED ITEMS

PEOPLE AND COMPANIES ARE FINDING WAYS TO TAKE OLD STUFF FROM TRASHED TO FABULOUS. HERE ARE SOME TOTAL TRANSFORMATIONS OF RECYCLED ITEMS.

Running shoes → Running tracks

NATIONAL GEOGRAPHIC KIDS MAGAZINE HOLDS THE WORLD RECORD FOR THE LARGEST COLLECTION OF SNEAKERS TO BE RECYCLED: 16,407 SHOES.

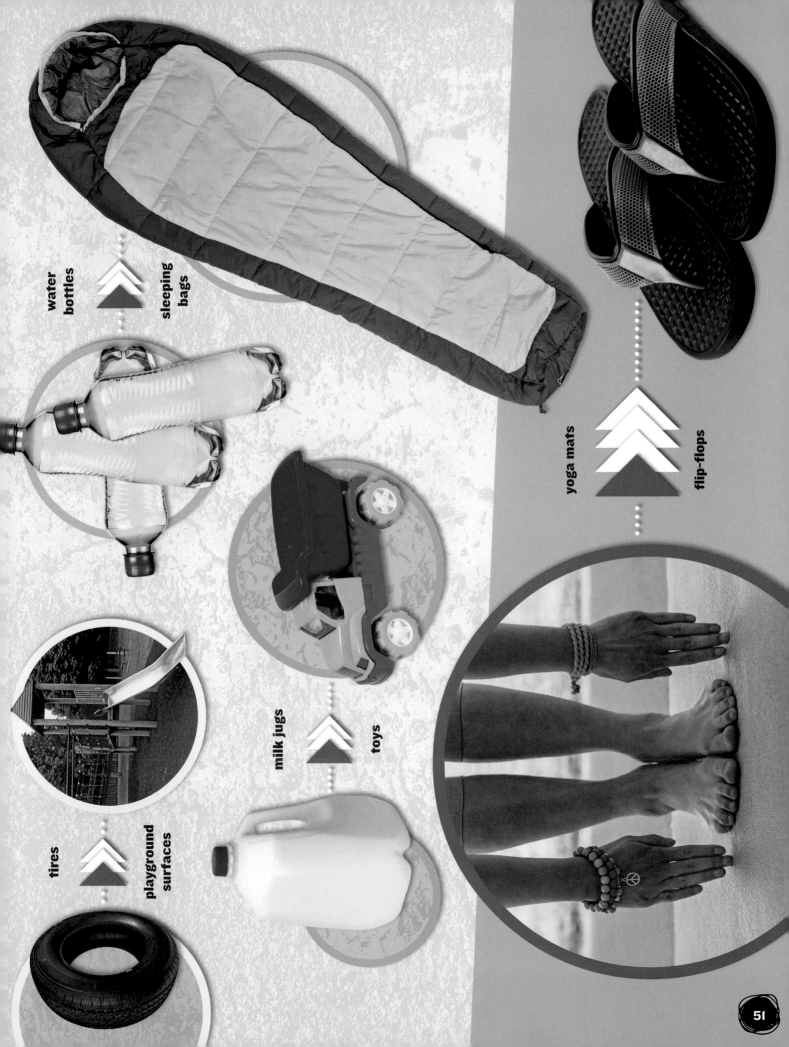

water
bottles

sleeping
bags

yoga mats

flip-flops

milk jugs

toys

tires

playground
surfaces

Waste on Wheels
Where: Oakland, California, U.S.A.
Why It's Wacky: This colorful mini mobile home was created out of recycled rubbish like bed frames, washing machine doors, and car parts.

What a Dish
Where: Huntsville, Texas, U.S.A.
Why It's Wacky: Transparent baking-dish lids double as skylights and windows in this home built from materials hauled out of trash heaps or picked up from the side of the road.

Deck the Walls
Where: Brighton, England, U.K.
Why It's Wacky: You won't go cold in this home, thanks to insulation made of 20,000 toothbrushes, thousands of floppy discs and DVD cases, and two tons (1.8 MT) of denim waste.

Ship It
Where: London, England, U.K.
Why It's Wacky: Old shipping containers have been transformed into colorfully chic condos in this riverfront complex fittingly known as "Container City."

Bottled Up
Where: Cornwall, England, U.K.
Why It's Wacky: Hundreds of old plastic bottles make up the walls and roof of this greenhouse located in an ecological park.

WACKY RECYCLED HOUSES

WOULD YOU LIVE HERE? THESE HOUSES— MADE MOSTLY OF JUNK—ARE ANYTHING BUT DUMPS.

Upcycled Abode
Where: Taos, New Mexico, U.S.A.
Why It's Wacky: This off-the-grid "earthship" dwelling features a foundation laid with used tires and walls constructed with cans and plastic bottles.

CAN YOU RECYCLE THAT?

GUESS WHAT BELONGS IN YOUR HOUSEHOLD RECYCLING BIN AND WHAT HAS TO BE TOSSED OR REUSED. ARE THESE ITEMS RECYCLABLE?

A Candy wrapper

B Juice squeeze pouch

C Laundry jug

D Pizza box

E Paper coffee cup

WHERE ARE THE TUNA CANS RECYCLED?

THAT'S A WRAP!

Don't just trash those unrecyclable wrappers and other items. Collect them and send them to TerraCycle, which repurposes hard-to-recycle materials. The group gathers everything from empty tape dispensers to toothpaste tubes to candy wrappers and repurposes them into new things, like purses and baskets. Want to learn more? Ask a parent for permission to visit the group's website at terracycle.com.

Recycling **RULES MAY VARY BY CITY AND COUNTRY.** Be sure to check your area's guidelines before you **TOSS YOUR STUFF.**

YOU CAN BUY A GREETING CARD THAT WILL GROW INTO WILD-FLOWERS AFTER YOU PLANT IT.

G **Polystyrene food container**

F **Potato chip bag**

55

CHAPTER 4

FOOD (WASTE) FOR THOUGHT

WHILE FOOD SCRAPS REPRESENT JUST A SMALL PORTION OF THE WORLD'S TRASH, THEY ARE BECOMING A BIG PROBLEM. NOT ONLY IS UNEATEN FOOD A HUGE WASTE OF MONEY—EXPERTS SAY THAT IN THE UNITED STATES ALONE, MORE THAN $160 BILLION WORTH OF FOOD IS TOSSED IN THE TRASH EVERY YEAR—BUT IT'S ALSO BAD FOR THE ENVIRONMENT. IN FACT, IF GLOBAL FOOD WASTE WERE A COUNTRY, IT WOULD BE THE THIRD LARGEST GENERATOR OF GREENHOUSE GASES IN THE WORLD BEHIND CHINA AND THE UNITED STATES. HERE'S THE SCOOP ON FOOD WASTE AND HOW SOME PEOPLE ARE VOWING TO PREVENT IT.

8 FOOD WASTE FACTS TO CHEW ON

A U.S. FAMILY OF FOUR **TRASHES** AN AVERAGE OF NEARLY **$1,500 WORTH OF EDIBLE FOOD** A YEAR.

A CAFÉ IN **LIVERPOOL, ENGLAND, U.K.,** OFFERS MEALS MADE ENTIRELY OUT OF **DISCARDED FOOD.**

FOOD-SHARING APPS ALLOW **CHARITIES** TO USE **SOCIAL MEDIA** TO COLLECT EXCESS GOODS FROM **BAKERIES** AND **RESTAURANTS.**

SOME **2.5 MILLION TONS** (2.3 MILLION MT) OF **FISH** IS **DISCARDED** IN THE **NORTH ATLANTIC** AND THE **NORTH SEA** ANNUALLY.

THINK IT'S NO BIG DEAL TO TOSS OUT THAT OLD SANDWICH? THINK AGAIN. HERE, WE UNCOVER THE TRUTH ABOUT UNEATEN FOOD. APPROXIMATELY ONE-THIRD OF FOOD PRODUCED WORLDWIDE FOR PEOPLE IS EITHER LOST OR WASTED.

A U.K. SUPERMARKET CHAIN ADMITTED TO **TOSSING 55,000 TONS** (49,000 MT) OF **FOOD** FROM ITS **STORES IN ONE YEAR.**

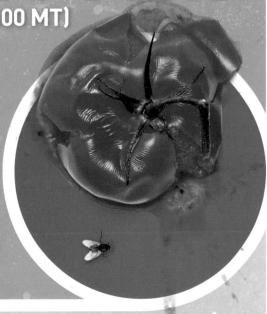

MORE **FOOD** REACHES **LANDFILLS** THAN **ANY OTHER** SINGLE SOLID-WASTE MATERIAL.

THE FOOD **WASTED** IN THE UNITED STATES **EACH YEAR**, COULD PROVIDE DAILY BREAKFAST, LUNCH, AND **DINNER** FOR **172 MILLION PEOPLE.**

MORE THAN ONE-QUARTER OF ALL **FRESH TOMATOES** IN THE UNITED STATES ARE **TOSSED** BEFORE THEY'RE **SOLD.**

THE AVERAGE PERSON **THROWS AWAY** MORE THAN **HALF A POUND** (0.2 kg) OF **FOOD A DAY.**

OVER THE COURSE
OF A YEAR,
THAT WOULD TOTAL...

60
LARGE BOTTLES OF SODA

190
LOAVES OF BREAD

120
PIZZAS

960
HAMBURGERS

LANDFILL LUNCH

A team of CHEFS served a meal made entirely out of FOOD WASTE to a group of high-ranking WORLD LEADERS dining at the UNITED NATIONS.

THE TRUTH BEHIND THE TRASH

In an effort to highlight the growing concern of food waste, two prominent chefs—including former White House chef Sam Kass—whipped up a meal made from often overlooked ingredients for a group of world leaders dining at the United Nations. Choosing food that would have otherwise ended up in landfills and ultimately emitted potent greenhouse gases, the meal included a vegetable burger made of pulp left over from juicing fruit and cucumber ends removed by the pickle industry to make perfectly shaped pickle slices.

And these chefs are not the only foodies picking through leftovers. Around the world, people are adopting the garbage-to-plate philosophy. There are cheeses being made out of excess steamed milk from coffee shops, crackers made from stale bread, and desserts consisting of cherry pulp, cocoa bean shells, and leftover nut skins. Whether or not trash cooking will take off as a culinary trend, it's definitely giving diners some, uh, food for thought.

IN THE U.S., KIDS THROW AWAY UP TO 40 PERCENT OF THEIR LUNCH EVERY DAY.

AT A RESTAURANT IN BRIGHTON, ENGLAND, YOU CAN ORDER THIS DECADENT RISOTTO DISH, WHICH IS MADE FROM FOOD WASTE!

DUMPSTER DINING

WOULD YOU EAT OUT OF THE TRASH? SOME PEOPLE DO—AND ARE PROUD OF IT.

These are professionals! Don't try this on your own.

WHO: Freegans

WHAT: People who **purposefully pick food** out of **Dumpsters** as a statement against **excessive food waste**

WHERE: Around the world; mostly in **large urban cities** like **New York, Los Angeles,** and **London**

ALTHOUGH DUMPSTER DIVING IS LEGAL (EXCEPT WHERE PROHIBITED BY LOCAL LAWS), FREEGANS USUALLY GO FORAGING LATE AT NIGHT TO AVOID ATTENTION.

Some freegans can gather up to **$1,000 worth of discarded food** in just **30 minutes** of foraging.

Freegans feast on **moldy cheese** (by scraping off the moldy parts) and **mushy vegetables,** but they pass on **discolored, stinky meat** and **rotten produce.**

a CURIOUS Harvest
the Practical Art of Cooking Everything

The movement inspired a **cookbook,** which includes recipes for turning **old veggies into soup stock.**

SOME FREEGAN ORGANIZATIONS OFFER TRASH TOURS THAT TEACH PEOPLE HOW AND WHERE TO FIND THE BEST STUFF AVAILABLE.

HOW COMPOSTING IS BECOMING COOL

By now, you know the importance of reducing the amount of food you throw away. But what about the old, icky stuff you just have to get rid of? Like that lettuce that's been stashed in the back of your fridge for months or the rotten bananas beginning to attract fruit flies? The most eco-friendly answer is composting: turning your food scraps into fertilizer for your yard or your plants. Large-scale composting centers can be found near many major cities; in some urban areas, like San Francisco, California, U.S.A., composting food waste is mandatory. Experts hope the trend continues, as a nationwide composting program could reduce our greenhouse emissions by up to 20 percent.

So how does composting work? Most of the food we waste—like eggshells, watermelon rinds, apple cores, and half-eaten bananas—is high in moisture and nitrogen. Once those scraps are mixed with "green" and "brown" material (dead leaves, dried pine needles, grass clippings, shredded newspaper,

Take a look inside a typical backyard composting bin.

or cardboard), and exposed to air, sunlight, and water, microbes and fungi in the soil will begin to break down the waste until it turns into compost. This takes only a matter of months. You can then use it as a natural fertilizer.

Seems simple enough, but is it catching on? Currently, just about 3 percent of Americans compost their food waste, citing the ick factor as the reason they shy away from saving their scraps. But many pro-compost organizations are trying to make it more mainstream. There are services that pick up your discarded food for you, and even companies that sell mini composters for people with limited space. Composting is also the norm on many college campuses, with cafeterias including special bins just for food waste. It's a slow-growing trend, but one that just may take off. And because of its many eco-friendly features, the hope is that one day, composting buckets will be just as common as recycling bins at homes across the world.

National Geographic Explorer Dr. T. H. Culhane and young scientist Meredith Puffer, age six, celebrate the installation of their hand-built household biodigester.

WHAT IN THE WORMS?

Aside from being small, slimy, and slithery, red worms are also composting kings. In fact, vermicomposting (that's the official name for worm composting) is considered one of the most effective ways to break down food waste and other organic material. How? Just place the wiggly worms in your composting bin, and they'll feast on your food scraps. Then their own waste becomes nutrient-rich soil you can collect and use on your plants. Worm poop to grow your garden? Genius!

THE BIG DEAL ABOUT BIODIGESTERS

Picture this: You're cleaning out the fridge after your family's weeklong vacation. So far, you've got a heap of past-their-prime leftovers, a few veggie scraps, and some rotten fruit. Oh, there's half a gallon of spoiled milk, too. No worries. Just toss it all in your backyard biodigester and head inside. By dinnertime, you could be preparing supper with gas produced from those stinky leftovers.

Sound like something from the future? Well, according to Dr. Thomas H. Culhane—a National Geographic emerging explorer, and part of the team behind the HomeBiogas system—the future is now. "Biodigesters don't just reduce food waste, they eliminate it," he says. "At my home, 100 percent of my organic waste goes into my home biodigester. I never have to take out the garbage."

Here's how it works: Once you toss your food scraps in the tank and seal it up, bacteria in the digester decomposes the organic material and produces enough clean energy to fuel three hours of cooking. Turn a spigot on the side of the tank and release the remains of your waste, which can be used as liquid fertilizer. That's one way to make your garden grow—and to reduce your family's carbon footprint!

MEET A FOOD-WASTE WARRIOR

Tristram Stuart believes no food should go to waste. And he's come up with creative ways to repurpose fruits, veggies, and other items from being tossed in the trash. Through his Feeding the 5000 campaign, Stuart serves massive meals made of surplus stock from farms, plus bruised or nicked produce deemed too ugly to sell in stores. The goal? To use some of the meals to serve the needs of more than one billion hungry people around the world—while reducing the amount of food we throw away every day.

Q: Have you always been an advocate against food waste?

A: I raised pigs on my parents' farm as a teenager and fed them with old food from local stores and bakeries. I soon noticed that most of the food was still good enough for humans to eat; the bread from the baker was better than what we bought at the store. As I became more and more aware about food waste's enormous environmental impact, I began campaigning for the issue.

Q: How did you get people on board with your cause?

A: I took people around to the back of grocery stores and showed them just how much we throw away—fruits and vegetables that may not be cosmetically perfect, but are perfectly good to eat. I didn't have to do much convincing after that.

Tristram Stuart grew up feeding the pigs on his farm with leftover and discarded food.

Sign the Pledge! Visit feedbackglobal.org to support the end to global food waste.

Q: **What have been the biggest achievements since you started your efforts?**

A: Today, there are major food corporations agreeing that it's unacceptable to throw so much away, and the United States recently announced a food waste reduction goal, calling for a 50 percent reduction by 2030. In the United Kingdom, food waste has been reduced by 21 percent—it's very difficult to find a more impactful environmental movement.

Foods that may not look pretty can still be good to eat.

Q: **What can we do to fight food waste starting at home?**

A: Anyone can take that slightly brown banana and turn it into a smoothie instead of tossing it, or make soups out of leftovers. But you also have the power to call the industry into account as well. It can be as simple as going into your local grocery store and asking about how much they are throwing away. Or you can get involved in any of the organizations that collect the discarded food and provide them to the needy, like food banks or food pantries. You can also sign a pledge to reduce food waste on my website, then share it with others.

EAT IT OR TOSS IT?

These are general guidelines, but you should always check with an adult!

POTATO WITH TUBERS OR SPROUTS?

ANSWER: Toss it! If something's growing on your spuds, get rid of them right away. Eating tubers or sprouts can be poisonous.

MOLDY CHEESE?

ANSWER: Eat it! Check with a parent, but as long as it's a firm cheese, like Cheddar or Swiss, simply cutting at least a half inch (1.3 cm) around the mold will make it as good as new.

MOLDY GRAPES?

ANSWER: Toss them! Mold can penetrate soft foods and make you sick. So if your fruit is fuzzy, throw the whole bunch in your composting bin.

THE UNITED STATES IS AIMING TO REDUCE FOOD WASTE BY 50 PERCENT BY 2030.

EGGS THREE WEEKS PAST THEIR EXPIRATION DATE?

ANSWER: Eat them! Check with a parent, but eggs are usually still good up to five weeks post-expiration. Not sure? Put them in a bowl of water. If the eggs sink, they're good.

STINKY MEAT?

ANSWER: Toss it! Anytime your raw meat has an odd odor or looks slimy, be smart and send it to the trash.

FRANCE IS THE FIRST COUNTRY TO BAN SUPERMARKET FOOD WASTE—ALL STORES MUST DONATE LEFTOVER FOOD

WILTED LETTUCE?

ANSWER: Eat it! Tossing wilted leaves in ice water will perk them up.

SOUR MILK?

ANSWER: Cook with it! Pasteurized milk that's gone sour is unlikely to make you sick. But you may not like the taste. It's best to use it as a substitute for buttermilk in pancake and biscuit recipes. (See page III for a recipe for sour milk pancakes!)

CHAPTER 5

DIRTY WORK

THEY ARE ICKY JOBS—BUT SOMEONE'S GOT TO DO THEM! AROUND THE WORLD, MANY PEOPLE GET THEIR HANDS DIRTY ON THE DAILY AND MAKE A LIVING DEALING WITH THE STUFF WE DUMP. WHETHER IT'S COLLECTING THE TRASH FROM YOUR STREET OR MAKING MASTERPIECES FROM JUNK, HERE ARE THE CRAZIEST—AND COOLEST—WAYS PEOPLE WORK WITH WASTE. MOST WASTE COLLECTORS DO THE IMPORTANT JOB OF KEEPING THE STREETS CLEAN AND SANITARY, BUT SOME INNOVATORS ARE ALSO FINDING NEW WAYS TO TAKE OUT THE TRASH.

THE WORLD'S MOST DANGEROUS JOB

A MOTORIZED TRASH CAN EQUIPPED WITH A POWERFUL ENGINE ONCE CLOCKED SPEEDS TOPPING 90 MILES AN HOUR (145 KM/H).

GARBAGE COLLECTORS are more likely to get INJURED on the job than POLICE OFFICERS.

THE TRUTH BEHIND THE TRASH: WHY SO RISKY?

It may be tough to believe that your friendly neighborhood garbage collector has a higher chance of getting hurt on the job than a firefighter battling a burning building. But according to recent studies, garbage collectors are twice as likely to be injured as other workers. Why? Besides falling and coming into contact with hazardous chemicals, you can also blame impatient, distracted drivers. Because a trash truck stops so much, it's not unusual for a car to try to zip around it while it's temporarily parked. And if a collector—also known as a "hopper"—happens to be on the street, he or she faces the danger of being hit. Not to mention that the heavy lifting of trash and exposure to glass and other sharp objects can also contribute to serious injuries.

To stall the scary stats surrounding this career, concerned citizens are lobbying for laws to protect garbage collectors. In the United States, some states have passed a "Slow Down to Get Around" law, which requires drivers to decrease their speed as they pass a utility truck. Additionally, both garbage collectors and garbage truck drivers go through extensive training to ensure their safety while doing this important job.

GARBAGE COLLECTING IS CONSIDERED RISKIER THAN FIREFIGHTING, PILOTING A PLANE, AND CONSTRUCTION WORK.

TRASH MADE ME RICH

IN ONE YEAR, THIS PROFESSIONAL DUMPSTER DIVER COULD MAKE $250,000 SELLING STUFF HE FOUND IN THE TRASH.

HE ALSO DONATES MANY OF HIS FINDS—INCLUDING WORKING COMPUTERS—TO NEIGHBORHOOD KIDS AND LOCAL CHARITIES.

WHO: Matt Malone

WHAT: Professional Dumpster Diver

WHERE: Austin, Texas, U.S.A.

COOLEST FIND: A collection of original paintings of famous boxer Muhammad Ali, worth more than $1,000 each

"On the whole, **humans are wasteful.** That will never change. So there's always going to be **more stuff** for me to find."

"Once, I found a bunch of **art supplies** at a craft store and took them home even though I'd **never** painted. Now, **I love to paint.**"

"I don't go to Dumpsters near restaurants. **I don't want to deal with food.** Dumpsters behind office supply stores, furniture stores, and electronics stores hardly ever have anything **gross** in them."

"A lot of the **furniture in my house** came from a Dumpster. I've also found **watches, computers, and TVs.**"

"One of my most fun finds? Over **200,000 tickets** from a Dumpster behind an **arcade.** I went back in, told them I found the tickets, and they still let me trade them in for prizes. **I 'bought' a guitar with those tickets.**"

"I regularly run into the same **raccoon** in one particular Dumpster. But **we have an agreement:** He doesn't bother me if I don't bother him."

Go Fish: This giant blue marlin is made of plastic debris—including toothbrushes, bottle caps, and bottles—all collected from the shores of Oregon, U.S.A.

After Party: A gallery cleaning crew mistook this art installation—made with glass bottles, confetti, and a party banner—for actual garbage. (Luckily, the artists found it stashed in a bag before it was gone for good.)

Having a Ball: For this stunning photo, an artist spent four months collecting 769 washed-up soccer balls along beaches around the world.

Going Ape: 7,500 coat hangers were used to make this larger-than-life gorilla, the world's largest art installation made of coat hangers.

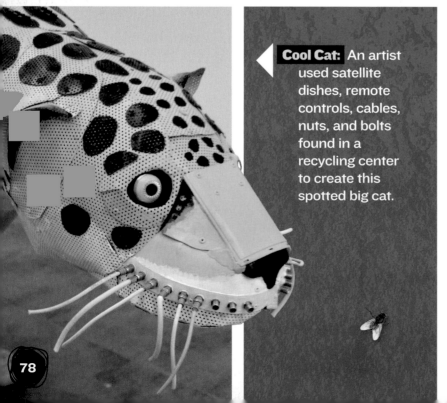

Cool Cat: An artist used satellite dishes, remote controls, cables, nuts, and bolts found in a recycling center to create this spotted big cat.

Trash People: Hundreds of life-size sculptures made of crushed soda cans, old computer parts, bottles, and more line a lake in the Swiss Alps. The work of German artist HA Schult, this parade of trash people is a statement about the excessive amount of trash humans throw away every day.

GARBAGE ART!

HOW SOME ARTISTS TURN WASTE INTO WOW-WORTHY WORKS OF ART

Boxed Up: More than 1,400 of these cubes of trash picked up from New York City streets have been sold in 30 countries around the world.

MEET A TRASH ACTIVIST

When Asher Jay was a little girl, she used to go door-to-door in her neighborhood getting people to sign petitions for beach cleanups and other environmental causes. Today, as a National Geographic Emerging Explorer, Asher has taken her passion for a clean planet to the next level. Here's more about this creative conservationist.

Q: How did you first get involved in waste awareness?

A: As a kid, I remember being so sad whenever I encountered litter, especially on the beach. I hated seeing pristine landscapes sullied by things that didn't belong there. Later, when I started working in fashion, I saw waste in the other way. Any fabric that wasn't used, or any clothes that didn't sell, would just get thrown away. It's a vicious cycle.

National Geographic Emerging Explorer Asher Jay also advocates for other important global issues, like big cat conservation.

Asher Jay has also used her art to put a spotlight on causes like protecting tigers from habitat loss.

Q: So what did you decide to do about it?

A: It really all began during a trip to Kenya. When I arrived, I watched in horror as zebras munched on food packaging and stepped around diapers and cigarette butts. So every day for three months, I filled up bags of garbage and gave them to the park rangers. It was my responsibility as a citizen of this planet, and I wanted to make people more conscious and cognizant of this issue.

Q: What about your work as an artist?

A: I took some of the trash home with me from Kenya and incorporated it into art inspired by African animals. In one painting, the giraffes' patches were replaced with labels of trash. I've also made art out of fabric waste, and I've created montages out of debris I found on the shorelines. Now I'm working on an installation with a crude-oil barrel picked up on the beach. I've become

the girl who collects garbage. It's a very powerful medium for an artist.

Q: What tips do you have for kids who may want to follow in your footsteps?

A: It doesn't have to be some major project. Pick one thing you're passionate about and take ownership of it. Never underestimate your impact, especially when you're young. You have tremendous capacity to make big changes that will directly affect your future.

IN TUNE WITH TRASH

WHAT: Recycled Orchestra

WHERE: Cateura, Paraguay

WHO: Kids from this poor city have gained **worldwide fame** by playing **instruments** created completely out of **recycled materials.**

MEMBERS HAVE GONE ON TO PLAY WITH PROFESSIONAL ORCHESTRAS.

Recycled Orchestra's director, Favio Chavez, shows off two of the instruments made with recycled materials found in a garbage dump.

Emerging from a tiny town built on a landfill, the Recycled Orchestra of Cateura, Paraguay, has become famous for its unique instruments and amazing sound. The young orchestra members—who make music on tin can cellos and cardboard violins—have performed with famous rock bands, played for the Queen of Spain, and are inspiring other recycled orchestras around the world.

Discarded x-rays and trash cans are transformed into percussion drums.

Oil drums, water pipes, spoons, packing crates, tin cans, and bottle caps are some of the recycled materials used to make the instruments.

The orchestra is featured in an award-winning documentary called Landfill Harmonic.

Recycled Orchestra musicians range in age from 12 to 18.

THE IDEA FOR THE ORCHESTRA STARTED AS A WAY TO KEEP KIDS FROM PLAYING IN THE LANDFILL.

WHAT IN THE WORLD?

A

THESE PHOTOS SHOW CLOSE-UP VIEWS OF COMMON THINGS FOUND IN THE TRASH AND RECYCLING BINS. UNSCRAMBLE THE LETTERS TO IDENTIFY WHAT'S IN EACH PICTURE. BONUS: USE THE HIGHLIGHTED LETTERS TO SOLVE THE RIDDLE BELOW. (STUMPED? FLIP THIS BOOK TO FIND THE ANSWERS ON THE BOTTOM OF THE PAGE.)

LEAREC OXB

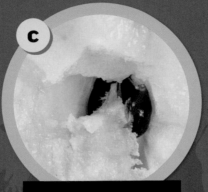

MUNALUIM ANC

PEPLA CERO

TLAISPC GAB

NBAANA LEPE

FECOFE PUC

KLIM UGJ

REAPP SLOTWE

RAPNESWPE

BONUS RIDDLE

Hint: Which bug gobbles up trash?

Answer: THE _ _ _ _ _ _ _ _ _ _

CHAPTER 6

THE FUTURE OF GARBAGE

TECHNOLOGY IS CONSTANTLY SHIFTING THE WAY WE DO THINGS, FROM HOW WE CHAT WITH FRIENDS TO HOW WE LEARN AT SCHOOL. AND THE WAY WE DEAL WITH TRASH IS NO EXCEPTION. FROM ROBOTS PICKING UP YOUR NEIGHBORHOOD TRASH TO SMARTCANS THAT DO THE DIRTY WORK FOR YOU, HERE'S A GLIMPSE OF GARBAGE IN THE FUTURE— AND THE AWESOME INNOVATIONS ALREADY HAPPENING TODAY. THESE AREN'T YOUR BASIC BINS! AS TECHNOLOGY BECOMES MORE ADVANCED, SO DO OUR TRASH CANS. HERE ARE SEVEN TRULY INNOVATIVE RECEPTACLES THAT ARE CHANGING THE WAY WE GET RID OF OUR WASTE.

7 EXTREME TRASH CANS

IN **BARCELONA**, SPAIN, SENSORS ON **SMART TRASH CANS** REMOTELY ALERT CLEANERS WHEN THEY'RE **FULL** USING WIRELESS LINKS.

THE **BRUNO** SMARTCAN **TEXTS YOU** WHEN IT'S TIME TO **TAKE OUT THE TRASH—** AND WHEN YOU NEED TO **BUY MORE BAGS.**

THESE AREN'T YOUR BASIC BINS! HERE ARE SEVEN TRULY INNOVATIVE GARBAGE CANS THAT ARE CHANGING THE WAY WE GET RID OF OUR WASTE.

SOME **SOLAR-POWERED** TRASH CANS ON **NEW YORK CITY** SIDEWALKS ALSO DOUBLE AS **WI-FI** ▶ **HOTSPOTS.**

IN **ISTANBUL,** TURKEY, SOME RECYCLING BINS DISPENSE **KIBBLE** FOR **STRAY DOGS** EVERY TIME YOU **PITCH A PLASTIC BOTTLE.**

OUR SOLAR TRASH COMPACTOR TOTALLY CRUSHES IT

THIS **WASTE BIN ON WHEELS** HAS **SENSORS** TO TRACK TRASH AS YOU TOSS IT, QUICKLY **MOVING TO CATCH IT** BEFORE IT HITS THE GROUND.

YOU CAN **BROWSE THE LATEST HEADLINES** FROM **LCD SCREENS** ON THE SIDE OF SOME **TRASH "PODS"** IN **LONDON,** ENGLAND, WHICH ALSO **SEPARATE RECYCLABLES FOR YOU.**

ATTACH THE **GENICAN GADGET** TO YOUR GARBAGE CAN AND IT SCANS **BAR CODES** OF ITEMS AS THEY'RE TOSSED, **AUTOMATICALLY UPDATING YOUR GROCERY LIST** WITH THE STUFF YOU'VE RUN OUT OF.

RUNNING ON RUBBISH

WHAT: A **car** that runs on **bioethanol fuel**

WHO: **Michihiko Iwamoto**, a Japanese **recycling activist** and **inventor**

WHERE: **Tokyo, Japan**

WHY: To **increase awareness** of **recycling** and **renewable energy** in Japan

This is a replica of the fictional car featured in the original *Back to the Future* movie. (The car in the movie also runs on trash.)

A JAPANESE INVENTOR CUSTOMIZED THIS DELOREAN TO BE POWERED IN PART BY BIOFUEL CREATED FROM OLD T-SHIRTS AND JEANS.

A TEENAGE GIRL IN EGYPT IS DEVELOPING A WAY TO TURN PLASTIC BOTTLES INTO BIOFUEL.

FAST FACTS

To make the **bioethanol from old clothes,** cotton fibers are broken down during a fermentation process and turned into energy.

It cost Iwamoto **$40,000** just to **ship the car** from the United States to Japan.

In Japan alone, some **two million tons** (1.8 million MT) of clothes and other fibers are **thrown away** each year.

Some companies, like Toyota, are **developing cars** that run on **fuel generated** by **garbage.**

What: Frozen Yogurt Pearls
Why It's Cool: These small frozen yogurt balls, encased in a fruit-flavored edible outer layer that's similar to a grape's skin, let you eat your dessert—and the package, too.

What: Package-Free Shopping
Why It's Cool: Original Unverpackt, a German grocer, is the first no-packaging store in Berlin. Shoppers fill their own reusable jars and bags with spices and pasta, which are all stored in glass containers.

What: Compostable Coffee Pods
Why It's Cool: Unlike most single-serve coffee pods, which aren't recyclable, the PūrPod100 is made from renewable, bio-based, or natural, materials that are 100 percent compostable.

What: Edible Water Bottles
Why It's Cool: Thirsty and hungry? You're in luck with these water blobs encased in a clear material made mostly of seaweed.

What: Sustainable Expanding Bowls
Why It's Cool: Pour hot water over these pretty packages from Innventia, and not only does the freeze-dried food inside cook, but the wrapper blossoms into a bio-degradable bowl.

THE TOTAL PACKAGE

WHEN IT COMES TO STUFF WE USE EVERY DAY, EXCESS PACKAGING IS A BIG PROBLEM. PLASTIC WRAPPERS, CONTAINERS, PAPER CARTONS, AND CARDBOARD BOXES FILL UP LANDFILLS FASTER THAN ANY OTHER TYPE OF TRASH. ONE STUDY EVEN SHOWS THAT THE AVERAGE ADULT THROWS AWAY HIS OR HER OWN WEIGHT IN PACKAGING EVERY MONTH. SO WHAT CAN WE DO ABOUT THIS PACKAGING PROBLEM? HERE'S HOW SOME COMPANIES ARE HOPING TO CURB IT.

What: Sugar Tubes
Why It's Cool: Some cosmetics come in tubes made from sugarcane, an eco-friendly alternative to plastic packaging.

What: Plantable Cups
Why It's Cool: Bury your cup in the ground and it'll grow flowers or trees, thanks to seeds embedded in its bio-degradable material.

ROAR FACTS

ROBOTS MAY SOON BE HAULING GARBAGE FROM YOUR HOUSE. A TEAM IS DEVELOPING A ROBOT THAT WILL ROLL AROUND YOUR NEIGHBORHOOD AND PICK UP TRASH. CALLED ROAR (SHORT FOR ROBOT-BASED AUTONOMOUS REFUSE HANDLING), THE ROBOT WILL HAVE THE ABILITY TO LIFT AND EMPTY BINS INTO THE BACK OF A GARBAGE TRUCK.

SOME GARBAGE TRUCKS ALREADY USE AUTOMATIC ARMS TO LIFT AND EMPTY BINS.

ROAR!

No more banging! The wheeled robots are being designed to **quietly** and **discreetly** dump trash.

Drivers will control the bots from an onboard operating system on a **high-tech truck—no heavy lifting required!**

Special **sensors** enable ROAR to **immediately stop** if a child or a dog runs in front of it.

Another company is developing a robot that uses **cameras, 3-D scanning,** and **metal detectors** to separate recyclables from the garbage.

How does ROAR know where to go? First, an aerial drone **lifts off** from the roof of the garbage truck and **scans the area** to **locate** the cans. The drone then **sends signals** to ROAR telling it where to **find the bins.** Brilliant!

ROAR IS EQUIPPED WITH GPS, CAMERAS, AND A RADAR SYSTEM THAT ALLOWS IT TO NAVIGATE NEIGHBORHOODS.

RETHINKING
RECYCLING
AND TRASH

CUTTING-EDGE IDEAS TO CHANGE OUR WASTEFUL WAYS.

What to do with those **old milk jugs?** With the still-in-development **RecycleBot,** you'll be able to instantly shred household plastics to create **supplies for 3-D printers.**

Soon, you may be sporting **new sneakers made out of trash.** Adidas—which is also working on a zero-waste shoe—is using **fishing nets** and **recycled ocean waste** to create eco-friendly shoes.

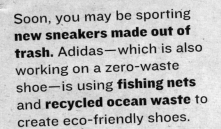

Some scientists are working on reducing **e-waste** by developing **biodegradable electronics** made from organic materials.

Think no one's paying attention to how much you recycle? They are if your bins are equipped with **radio-frequency identification (RFID) tags.** These high-tech tags enable garbage companies to **track and weigh your bins,** as well as gather other info—right down to **your personal recycling rate.**

No more sorting paper from plastic! New technology has led to the development of **single-stream recycling,** in which machines—equipped with **magnets** and special **sensors**—automatically separate recyclables.

Now you see it ... now you don't. Major cities, including New York, use **vacuum-powered underground tubes** to keep trash off the streets, silently **sucking up waste at 60 miles an hour** (96.5 km/h) and sending it to a collection and sorting facility.

AT 96 STORIES, IT'S THE TALLEST APARTMENT BUILDING IN THE WESTERN HEMISPHERE.

THE METAL TRASH CAN THAT INSPIRED IT ALL—ORIGINALLY DESIGNED IN 1905—NOW SELLS FOR $225!

INSPIRED BY A TRASH CAN

The **DESIGN** for this New York City skyscraper was **INSPIRED** by a **METAL WASTEBASKET.**

THE TRUTH BEHIND THE TRASH

Trash cans aren't usually the first things that pop into mind when you think of elegant, modern buildings. But one of Manhattan's newest high-rises was actually based on the design of a vintage metal wastebasket. According to the building's architect, the silver gridded exterior is a near replica of the column-like can. While the outside of the building may look a little like a trash bin, the interior is definitely not a dump: The cost to live in the penthouse is close to $100 million!

ARE YOU A GARBAGE GENIUS?

HOW MUCH DO YOU KNOW ABOUT TRASH? TAKE THIS QUIZ TO FIND OUT IF YOU'RE A GARBAGE GENIUS.

HEY! YOU BETTER NOT THROW AWAY THAT DOGGY BAG!

1 **True or false?**
Old landfills are often turned into parks or green spaces.

2 **What makes up the bulk of waste around the world?**
A. Newspapers
B. Plastic
C. Food scraps
D. Yard trimmings

3 **Some _____ zip(s) around at a rate that's 20 times the speed of sound.**
A. Garbage trucks
B. Motorized trash cans
C. Space trash
D. Trash robots

4 Which creepy crawlers can be used to help compost your food?

A. Crickets
B. Centipedes
C. Spiders
D. Worms

5 True or false?

Before the days of trash pickup and dumps, people used to throw their trash on the streets for animals to eat.

TRASH ISN'T JUST **FILTHY—** IT'S **FUNNY!** HERE ARE SOME **RUBBISH-THEMED RIDDLES** AND **JOKES** TO TRY OUT ON YOUR FRIENDS AND FAMILY.

Q. WHAT HAS FOUR WHEELS AND FLIES?

A. A GARBAGE TRUCK.

Q. WHAT DID THE GARBAGEMAN SAY AS HE WAS DIGGING THROUGH TRASH?

A. MAN, I'M DOWN IN THE DUMPS TODAY!

CHAPTER 7

TAKE OUT THE TRASH

WANT TO MAKE A DIFFERENCE WHEN IT COMES TO GARBAGE? FIND OUT ALL ABOUT HOW TO DO EVERYTHING FROM STARTING A BACKYARD COMPOST TO ORGANIZING A NEIGHBORHOOD CLEANUP. EVEN THE LITTLEST THINGS CAN ADD UP TO MAJOR CHANGES. SO WHAT ARE YOU WAITING FOR? START NOW! NOW THAT YOU'RE A WHIZ ON WASTE, IT'S TIME TO REALLY TAKE OUT THE TRASH.

compost dwy
compostables

≫ DO SOMETHING

Now that you've discovered just how much excess waste there is around the world, it's time for you to do something. Yes, you! Play a part in cleaning up the Earth, whether it's something small (like recycling) or much bigger (like creating awareness about this issue in your school and beyond). Here, we explore all the ways you can contribute to the cleanup—and how you can encourage others to think twice about tossing that piece of trash.

Where to begin? Start by checking out the items on this list. Or gather up a group of friends and brainstorm your own ways to reduce rubbish around your home and neighborhood. Then, get your parents and teachers on board. The more support you have from your community, the easier it will be to turn your ideas into actions.

Even something as simple as setting up recycling and composting bins at your local park can make a huge difference in reducing waste.

CHECKLIST: WHAT YOU CAN DO

☐ Clean up your neighborhood

☐ Reduce waste in your home

☐ Cut back on food waste

☐ Create a compost bin

☐ Repurpose your old stuff

CLEAN IT UP!

PICKING UP THE PLANET CAN START RIGHT ON YOUR STREET. HERE'S HOW TO ORGANIZE A NEIGHBORHOOD CLEANUP.

1 Pick a Location

Is there a local road that's **covered in rubbish?** Or a nearby beach just **swimming in litter?** Select a spot that really needs some **extra attention.**

2 Get Permission

Share your plan with your family. They may have ideas for how you can go about **organizing your efforts** or getting the word out about your event.

3 Save the Date

Look at your family's calendar and find a **free Saturday or Sunday** within the next couple of months. You'll want to give yourself **at least a few weeks** to prepare and give notice to your neighbors. Don't forget to **set a rain date** in the event of bad weather.

SAFETY FIRST! Make sure to **WEAR GLOVES** while you pick up to avoid contact with any hazardous material.

Never pick up **SHARP, RUSTY,** or **HEAVY** items. Spot something **POTENTIALLY DANGEROUS?** Make a note of its location and tell an adult.

For more tips on organizing a cleanup and staying safe, grab a parent and go online to visit **Keep America Beautiful (kab.org).**

6 Give a Heads-Up

Once you have a **list of volunteers,** send a brief e-mail **reminding** them of the date and time with details on where to meet.

4 Get the Info Out

Put out signs or **hang flyers** with the date, location, and time of your cleanup around your neighborhood. Ask a parent to share the info on your neighborhood newsletter or on their **social media page.** Be sure to have volunteers **RSVP** to you (or a parent) with their e-mail address for quick correspondence later on.

5 Ask for Donations

Go to **nearby businesses** and ask if they can **donate to your cause.** The **hardware store** may offer garbage bags, plastic gloves, or tools; your **local bakery** may donate bagels and other snacks for the morning of the event. Your community **waste-management organization** may also offer supplies and other types of support.

7 Share Your Work

On cleanup day, be sure to **take plenty of pictures** (or have a friend snap some) to post online or include in an upcoming **community newsletter.** (Pssst: Your school or teacher would probably love to see some pics too!)

8 Show Appreciation

When the last piece of trash is all picked up? **Give a giant thanks to your cleaning crew.** Send out a recap e-mail detailing things like **how many bags of trash you hauled away** and the **number of volunteers** you had. Then start planning your next cleanup event!

REDUCE WASTE AT HOME

IT'S NOT JUST ABOUT THROWING LESS AWAY. WHEN IT COMES TO LIMITING THE TRASH THAT YOUR FAMILY PRODUCES, HERE'S HOW TO CUT BACK FROM TOP TO BOTTOM.

FOR DONATION
↓

Bulk Up

To eliminate some of the excess packaging piling up in landfills, **encourage your family to shop for snacks, cereal, and pasta in the bulk section of your grocery store** (if yours doesn't have any bulk items, check out a nearby natural food shop). Then, **store it all in reusable glass jars.**

Minimize Your Mail

Is your mailbox always full of catalogs? Talk to your family about **reducing junk mail** by visiting websites like **dmachoice.org** and **catalogchoice.org**.

Give Back

Recycle whatever—and whenever—you can. This includes clothes you've grown out of and old toys. Instead of sending them to the dump, **donate them to friends or family or to a local thrift store.**

ZERO-WASTE LUNCH!

The trash you create by **bringing lunch to school** every day can create as much as 100 pounds (45 kg) of garbage a year! Follow these tips to **leave less behind.**

Reach for Reusable

Instead of packing your sandwich and snacks in plastic bags, **use reusable containers or cloth sacks instead.** Same goes for your drink: Skip the juice boxes and opt for a refillable water bottle.

Bag It

Reduce the amount of plastic bags clogging up our trash and oceans by shopping with **reusable bags** instead.

Toss in Fruit

Pack an apple, a banana, or an orange. Fruit **fills you up in a healthy way,** plus there's **no need for extra packaging.** (Save the core, peels, and rinds for your **compost bin.**)

Nix Paper Napkins and Wipe Out Paper Towels

It's estimated that **17 trees are cut down for every ton (0.9 MT) of non-recycled paper.** Save some branches by bringing a **cloth napkin that you can wash and reuse.**

Clean up in an eco-friendly way by using **cloths instead of paper towels.** Make your own rags by cutting up old towels or clothes headed to the donation bin.

NO WASTE CHALLENGE!

Using these tips, keep track of the trash you toss. Every week, try to throw out less and less and see how much you can minimize your waste in a month. Some people have managed to put an entire year's worth of garbage in one jar. Can you beat that?

5 WAYS YOU CAN CURB FOOD WASTE RIGHT NOW

EAT WHAT YOU **HAVE.**

Before you complain that there's **"nothing to eat"** or ask your parents to **grab dinner out,** check out what's at home first. Help your family come up with ideas for what to make with **the food in your fridge or pantry.**

SMOOSH UP YOUR **FRUIT.**

Are your bananas **a bit brown?** Strawberries **a bit soft?** Toss them in a **smoothie** or make **muffins** with them.

KEEP TRACK OF WHAT YOU **TOSS.**

For a couple of weeks, **write down** all the food you and your family **throw away.** Look for patterns: **If you're dumping veggies** because they've gone bad, it's probably **better to buy less** in the first place.

SAVE THAT SOUR MILK!

Milk's gone bad? Don't dump it down the drain. You can still find a purpose for pasteurized sour milk, as long as it's not separated or clumpy. In fact, people have been using sour milk as a replacement for buttermilk, yogurt, or sour cream in recipes for centuries. So the next time you have some old milk lying around, why not whip up a batch of these pancakes? Just be sure a parent is around to help you out in the kitchen.

SOUR MILK PANCAKES

1 cup all-purpose flour
1 teaspoon baking powder
1/2 teaspoon baking soda
1 pinch salt
2 tablespoons maple syrup

1 cup sour milk
1/4 teaspoon vanilla
1 egg
1 tablespoon coconut oil, melted

1. Add flour, baking powder, baking soda, and a pinch of salt to a large mixing bowl.
2. In a separate, smaller bowl, whisk together maple syrup, milk, vanilla, egg, and oil.
3. Gently stir the wet mix into the dry ingredients.
4. To cook, melt 1 teaspoon coconut oil in a large frying pan or griddle. Add batter to the pan by the 1/4 cup. When the bubbles pop and make holes that don't disappear, flip, and cook until done.

GIVE IT AWAY.

Just can't stomach any more of those **leftovers** from your pizza party or a family meal? There's probably **someone out there** who's ready to gobble them up. Instead of throwing food away, pick up your smartphone (with your parent's permission, of course!). Apps like **Leftover Swap** connect "leftover givers" with "leftover takers" for a quick and easy way to **reduce food waste.** You can also look into **donating goods to a local soup kitchen or charity.**

PILE LESS ON YOUR PLATE.

Sure, you may feel starving, but **you can always get seconds!** Avoid taking **heaping portions** of food so you won't wind up throwing away what you **don't finish.**

CREATE A COMPOST!

DON'T LET THOSE FOOD SCRAPS SLIDE INTO YOUR TRASH CAN! FOOD COMPOSTING LOWERS YOUR CARBON FOOTPRINT BY REDUCING METHANE EMISSIONS FROM LANDFILLS. PLUS, YOU'LL CREATE A SPECIAL FERTILIZER THAT WILL HELP YOUR GARDEN GROW. HERE'S HOW TO CREATE YOUR OWN COMPOSTING BIN AT HOME.

1 **Talk to Your Family**

Composting is a family affair! You'll want everyone on board to make it all run smoothly.

2 **Buy a Bin**

To keep smells (and critters) away, you'll want to invest in a composting bin (a trash-can-size bucket with a lid) from a hardware store.

3 **Gather Your Greens (and Browns)**

To create the right reaction in your bin, you need a mix of greens (food waste, grass clippings) and browns (yard waste, newspapers). First, get together your browns, chopping or shredding the larger pieces.

4 Layer It

Add the browns to your bin, then put the greens on top. Keep the contents damp by lightly watering them with a hose or watering can.

5 Keep Turning

As you add stuff to your bin, be sure to have an equal amount of browns and greens, alternating between the layers. Turn or mix your bin every time you add more waste.

6 Time is Right

Depending on what's inside your bin and how often you turn the contents over, you'll likely have compost within a few months. You'll know it's ready when it's dark brown and crumbly and smells like soil—not rotting vegetables.

COMPOST THIS!

Yard waste (leaves, grass cuttings, weeds, sticks)
Eggshells
Fruit and vegetable peelings
Tea bags
Coffee grounds
Shredded paper and cardboard (cereal boxes, egg cartons)

LEAVE IT IN THE TRASH CAN

Meat, fish, and dairy products
Cooked foods
Tissues and napkins

WHO ARE YOU CALLING STINKY?

UPCYCLE
YOUR STUFF

Be sure to ask a parent for **PERMISSION** before you begin any project!

SIMPLE WAYS TO REPURPOSE ITEMS FOUND AROUND YOUR HOUSE

CATCH-IT!

TURN YOUR **EMPTY JUGS** INTO A **FUN GAME** FOR **TWO!**

MATERIALS:
Two large empty milk containers or laundry detergent jugs with handles
Scissors
Colorful masking tape or duct tape
Stickers, markers, and other embellishments

1
Thoroughly **wash** and **dry** your containers.

2
With a parent's help, use scissors to **carefully cut about three inches (7.6 cm) off the bottom** of each jug.

3
Use the tape to **cover the jugs' sharp edges.**

4
Customize the jugs by decorating them with more tape, stickers, or markers.

5
Let everything dry. Then grab a lightweight plastic or rubber ball and a friend, and **play catch!**

MINI BIN

CREATE YOUR OWN DESKTOP TRASH OR RECYCLING BIN USING AN OLD ICE-CREAM CONTAINER!

MATERIALS:
- A large empty ice-cream or popcorn container
- Wrapping paper with a cool design
- Scissors
- Tape
- Stickers and other embellishments (optional)

1
Thoroughly **wash** and **dry** your container.

2
With a parent's help, **cut the wrapping paper** so that it **completely covers the outside** of the container.

3
Wrap the paper tightly around your container, carefully **folding and taping** the edges like you're wrapping a present.

4
If you want, **add stickers, ribbon, pom-poms, or other embellishments**—or just leave it as is.

5
Place the bin on your desk, your bathroom counter, or your dresser as an **easy-to-reach receptacle** for your recyclables or trash.

REPURPOSE A PLASTIC BOTTLE FOR SOME WILD WATER PLAY

MATERIALS:
Two-liter soda bottle
Thumbtack
Garden hose
Duct tape

2

Use the **duct tape** to **secure** your backyard **hose** to the **mouth of the bottle** and turn on the water.

1

Using the thumbtack, **punch a bunch of holes about one inch** (2.5 cm) **apart** along the length of the bottle. **Rotate** the bottle and continue punching holes on about three-quarters of it (you don't have to punch holes on the side that will be laying on the ground).

3

Run, get wet, **repeat!**

BE ON THE LOOKOUT FOR RAINBOWS CAUSED BY LIGHT BENDING IN THE WATER DROPLETS.

IF YOU WANT A HIGHER SPRAY, POKE FEWER HOLES IN THE BOTTLE. BUILDING PRESSURE MEANS BIGGER GEYSERS!

HOW TO REGROW VEGGIES FROM YOUR SCRAPS

Next time your mom or dad is about to **toss those extra veggie** bits into the trash or compost bin, **grab 'em!** Some vegetables have the ability to **regenerate their roots—**and grow a brand-new plant, sometimes within weeks. Here are the goods on **regrowing your food** from scraps.

LETTUCE

1. **Place leftover leaves** in a bowl with just a bit of water at the bottom.

2. Keep the bowl in a sunny spot and **mist the leaves** with water every other day.

3. After three or four days, you should start to **see sprouts** appearing on the old leaves. When this happens, **transplant the lettuce** into soil, keeping it moist.

4. Within **a few weeks,** you should have a new head of lettuce.

CELERY

1. **Take the base** of the bunch of celery, **rinse it,** and **place it** in a shallow container filled with warm water with the cut part facing upright.

2. **Leave it** on a sunny windowsill with the top exposed, changing the water every other day.

3. **Gently mist** the plant with a spray bottle filled with water every other day.

4. You should start to see **tiny yellow leaves** around the center of the base, which will grow thicker and turn dark green.

5. After about a week, **move the celery** to a planter or your garden and **cover it** with soil, leaving the leaf tips exposed. **Water well.** You should have celery stalks within a few months.

BASIL

1. **Cut several four-inch (10-cm) stems** from a bunch of basil, gently pulling most of the leaves off, but leaving the two small leaves on the top.

2. **Place the stems** in a water-filled glass, keeping it in a bright (but not too warm) spot.

3. **Replace the water** every other day. You should soon see **new roots** forming along the stems.

4. Once the roots are about two inches (5 cm) long, **plant the individual stems** in a pot, keeping it in an area that gets plenty of sunshine. Water regularly.

5. New shoots should emerge within a few weeks. **Pluck the leaves** as needed to top your pizza or add to your pasta.

POTATO

1. **Cut off** the eyes on your potatoes and **dry them out** overnight.

2. **Dig a four-inch** (10-cm) **hole** in soil and place the eyes facing up. Cover the hole.

3. Within a few weeks, you will see a **new potato plant** beginning to grow.

POTATO EYES

AVOCADO

1. Take a **clean avocado pit** and press four toothpicks into its center.

2. **Suspend the pit,** pointy-side up, in a glass filled about halfway with water.

3. **Store** in a sunny spot and change the water every day.

4. After a few weeks, stems will form.

5. Once the plant is 7 inches (18 cm) tall, plant it in a 10-inch (25-cm) pot.

6. Keep the plant in a **sunny spot,** and bring it indoors if it's cold.

Note:
Your avocado tree may not produce fruit, but it's still fun to watch it grow!

AFTERWORD

Now that you've read this book, hopefully you are more aware than ever of how trash impacts our planet. And maybe you're more fired up than ever to do your part to pick up waste, recycle right, and just be more aware of how your actions affect the Earth. Awesome! Now it's time to take action. Sure, it may not be convenient to save those food scraps for composting or hold on to that empty bottle until you find a recycling bin. But for every contribution you make, you **do** make a difference. You could be stopping one more piece of trash from making its way into our oceans. You could be saving an animal's life.

Even the smallest efforts you make to reduce waste in your world can lead to big changes. Think about it: One person turning off the lights may not make much of a difference in conserving energy, but if everyone turned off their lights after leaving a room, those actions would add up. The same is true when it comes to what we do with our waste. By committing to reducing waste at home and encouraging your friends and family to do the same, you can set an example for others to follow.

So share your knowledge! Together we can help shrink the staggering amount of trash we generate. It'll take all of us working together to save and protect our planet!

INDEX

Boldface indicates illustrations.

PHOTO CREDITS

Front cover: (UP LE), r.classen/Shutterstock; (UP RT), Sonsedska Yuliia/Shutterstock; (CTR), Skypixel/Dreamstime; (LE), Africa Studio/Shutterstock; (LO LE), ajt/Shutterstock; spine: Picsfive/Shutterstock; **back cover:** (UP LE), Callie Broaddus/NG Staff; (UP RT), Evan Lorne/Shutterstock; (LO LE), Callie Broaddus/NG Staff; (LO), Susan Schmitz/Shutterstock

Interior: 1, Picsfive/Shutterstock; 3, Sonsedska Yuliia/Shutterstock; 5 (UP RT), Jim West/Alamy Stock Photo; 5 (UP LE), Caters News Agency; 5 (CTR LE), Peter Yang/AUGUST; 5 (CTR RT), Photo courtesy Silo Brighton; 5 (LO RT), culture-images/Alamy Stock Photo; 6-7, Photomyeye/Dreamstime;

Chapter 1: 9 (LE), Callie Broaddus/NG Staff; 9 (RT), Susan Schmitz/Shutterstock; 10 (tape), Picsfive/Shutterstock; 10 (LO), Isselee/Dreamstime; 11 (food), V ra Kontríková/Dreamstime; 11 (glass), Bugtiger/Dreamstime; 11 (metals), Vitaly Kuzmin/Dreamstime; 11 (paper), Jirkaejc/Dreamstime; 11 (plastics), Photka/Dreamstime; 11 (textiles), Baloncici/Dreamstime.com; 11 (wood), Pumbal/Dreamstime; 11 (yard trimmings), Tadeusz Wejkszo/Dreamstime; 12-13 (UP), WestLight/iStockphoto/Getty Images; 12 (cockroaches), Meepoohya/Dreamstime; 13 (CTR), Uatp1/Dreamstime; 13 (LO), Vatikaki/Dreamstime; 14-15, Steve Mann/Dreamstime; 14 (paper scraps), picsfive/Shutterstock;14 (LE), Richard Thomas/Dreamstime; 14 (LO), Jonathan Vasata/Dreamstime; 15 (RT), a454/Shutterstock; 15 (UP LE), Maposee Soleh/Dreamstime; 16 (worms), Valentina Razumova/Shutterstock; 18 (LO CTR), Sheila Fitzgerald/Shutterstock; 18 (LO LE), Alexlmx/Dreamstime; 18 (UP LE), Péter Gudella/Dreamstime; 18 (UP RT), Duncan Noakes/Dreamstime; 18 (UP CTR), Anan Punyod/Dreamstime; 18 (LO RT), dcwcreations/Shutterstock; 19, Israel images/Alamy Images; 19 (UP RT), Backus Aerial Photography; 20 (UP LE), Leonid Yastremskiy/Dreamstime; 20 (CTR), Wellphotos/Dreamstime; 21 (UP RT), Wuka/Dreamstime; 21 (CTR LE), Igor Zavalskiy/Shutterstock; 21 (CTR RT), hxdbzxy/Shutterstock; 21 (LO LE), Chuyu/Dreamstime; 21 (LO RT), Ljupco Smokovski/Shutterstock; 22-23 (LO), Johnnydao/Dreamstime; 22 (CTR RT), Brad Calkins/Dreamstime; 22 (UP LE), Madrabothair/Dreamstime; 22 (UP RT), Mada Jimmy/Dreamstime; 23 (RT), Chris Curtis/Dreamstime; 23 (UP), hasrullnizam/Shutterstock;

Chapter 2: 25, NASA; 26 (CTR RT), Konstantin Faraktinov/Shutterstock; 26 (CTR RT), pudiq/Shutterstock; 26 (LE), Ganna Poltoratska/Dreamstime; 26 (RT), Dreamstime.com; 27 (CTR LE), Arnaldo Jr/Shutterstock; 27 (CTR LE), Akiyoko74/Dreamstime; 27 (CTR RT), Bjeayes/Dreamstime; 27 (LE), Jeffrey Banke/Dreamstime; 27 (RT), James Boardman/Dreamstime; 27 (CTR RT), hxdbzxy/Shutterstock; 28 (CTR), Eraldo Peres/AP Photo; 28 (LO), Anadolu Agency/Getty Images; 28 (UP), Spencer Platt/Getty Images; 28 (LO), Jim Osborn/AP Images; 28 (UP), Steve Marcus/Las Vegas

Sun/AP Images; 30, Peter Cripps/Alamy Images; 32 (UP), Paul Ives/Alamy; 32 (LO), Flip Nicklin/Minden Pictures; 32 (UP), Nicholas Eveleigh/Getty Images; 32 (UP LE), Chones/Shutterstock; 33 (UP), imagehub/Shutterstock; 33, Michel Porro/Contour/Getty Images; 34, Sergi Garcia Fernandez/Biosphoto/Minden Pictures; 34 (CTR), Nicholas Eveleigh/Getty Images; 34 (LO), Chones/Shutterstock; 36 (CTR), gualtiero boffi/Shutterstock; 36 (LE), NASA; 36 (RT), Andrey zVP/Shutterstock; 37, Naeblys/Shutterstock; 37, 3Dsculptor/Shutterstock; 37 (UP), Andrey Armyagov/Shutterstock; 38 (LO LE), Mariyana M/Shutterstock; 38 (UP RT), Stephanie Frey/Dreamstime; 39 (LO), Eric Isselee/Shutterstock; 39 (UP RT), Mike Flippo/Shutterstock;

Chapter 3: 41, Photo Courtesy Greg Kendall/ladailypost.com; 42 (LE), Phil Degginger/Alamy Stock Photo; 43 (LO), Citizen of the Planet/Alamy Stock Photo; 43 (LO RT), Fabrikacrimea/Dreamstime; 43 (UP RT), Juice Images/Alamy Stock Photo; 44 (LO CTR LE), Fredrik Vindelälv/Dreamstime; 44 (UP CTR LE), Jiri Hubatka/Alamy Stock Photo; 44 (CTR RT), Vacclav/Shutterstock; 44 (LO), Photoquest/Dreamstime; 44 (UP), blvdone/Shutterstock; 45 (LO), Robert Gilhooly/Alamy Stock Photo; 45 (UP), Luis Dafos/Alamy Stock Photo; 46 (LO), Sean Pavone/Dreamstime; 46 (UP), Scanrail/Dreamstime; 47 (LO), Rodrigo Kristensen/Shutterstock; 47 (UP), Chris Ratcliffe/Getty Images; 48 (LE), Radu Sigheti/Reuters; 48 (RT), Photo Courtesy TerraCycle; 48-49, Alexander Tamargo/Getty Images; 48 (CTR), Photo Courtesy Greg Kendall/ladailypost.com; 48-49, Caters News Agency; 49 (CTR RT), Courtesy of Austin-Mergold; 49 (LO RT), Dirty Sugar Photography; 49 (UP LE), Joao Sabino/Solent News/REX/Shutterstock; 49 (UP RT), Jamie Squire/Getty Images; 49 (LO), Jess Yu/Dreamstime; 50 (UP), Patrick Allen/Dreamstime; 50, Elisabeth Burrell/Dreamstime; 51 (LO CTR LE), Art Directors & TRIP/Alamy Stock Photo; 51 (CTR RT), Adrian Petrean/Dreamstime; 51 (UP CTR LE), Loongar/Dreamstime; 51 (LO LE), Igor Zakharevich/Dreamstime; 51 (LO RT), Poprotskiy Alexey/Shutterstock; 51 (UP LE), Zavgsg/Dreamstime; 51 (UP RT), Shyamalamuralinath/Shutterstock; 51 (CTR LE), Michael Stravato/The New York Times/Redux Pictures; 52 (LO CTR), Arcaid/UIG/Getty Images; 52 (LO LE), WENN Photos/Newscom; 52 (LO RT), Ashley Cooper/Getty Images; 52 (UP), Brian J Reynolds/Caters News; 52 (CTR LE), Africa Studio/Shutterstock; 53 (CTR LE), tanaphongpict/Shutterstock; 53 (LO), Ricardo DeAratanha/Getty Images; 53 (UP), John Minchillo/AP Images; 53 (CTR LE), Kitchner Bain/Dreamstime; 54 (LO CTR), Mariusz Blach/Dreamstime; 54 (CTR RT), Africa Studio/Shutterstock; 54 (UP CTR), Keith Bell/Dreamstime; 54 (LO RT), Deamles for Sale/Shutterstock; 54 (UP), Cultura Creative (RF)/Alamy Stock Photo; 54 (LO LE), Yalcin Sonat/Shutterstock; 55 (LO RT), 9george/Shutterstock; 55 (UP LE), Eyewave/Dreamstime; 55, Ian Allenden/Dreamstime;

Chapter 4: 57 (LO CTR), Arctic Images/Alamy Stock

TO MARK, MY TRASH AND RECYCLING MAN FOR LIFE. AND TO MY LITTLEST WASTE WARRIORS, EAMON, NORA, AND NELL: YOU REMIND ME EVERY DAY JUST HOW IMPORTANT IT IS TO PROTECT OUR PLANET TO ENSURE YOUR VERY BRIGHT FUTURES. —SWF

Since 1888, the National Geographic Society has funded more than 12,000 research, exploration, and preservation projects around the world. The Society receives funds from National Geographic Partners, LLC, funded in part by your purchase. A portion of the proceeds from this book supports this vital work. To learn more, visit natgeo.com/info.

NATIONAL GEOGRAPHIC and Yellow Border Design are trademarks of the National Geographic Society, used under license.

For more information, visit nationalgeographic.com, call 1-800-647-5463, or write to the following address:
National Geographic Partners
1145 17th Street N.W.
Washington, D.C. 20036-4688 U.S.A.

Visit us online at nationalgeographic.com/books

For librarians and teachers: ngchildrensbooks.org

More for kids from National Geographic: kids.nationalgeographic.com

For information about special discounts for bulk purchases, please contact National Geographic Books Special Sales: specialsales@natgeo.com

For rights or permissions inquiries, please contact National Geographic Books Subsidiary Rights: bookrights@natgeo.com

The publisher gratefully acknowledges the work and creativity of project manager and editor Ariane Szu-Tu, designers Amanda Larsen and Callie Broaddus, designer and illustrator Sanjida Rashid, photo editors Jeff Heimsath and Lisa Jewell, production editor Alix Inchausti, design production assistant Gus Tello, and Kaya Dengel for his arts and crafts contributions.

Art directed and designed by Callie Broaddus

Library of Congress Cataloging-in-Publication Data

Names: Flynn, Sarah Wassner, author. | National Geographic Society (U.S.)
Title: This book stinks! : gross garbage, rotten rubbish, and the science of trash / by Sarah Wassner Flynn.
Other titles: National Geographic kids.
Description: Washington, D.C. : National Geographic, [2017] | Series: National Geographic kids | Includes bibliographical references and index.
Identifiers: LCCN 2016030510| ISBN 9781426327308 (pbk. : alk. paper) | ISBN 9781426327315 (library binding : alk. paper)
Subjects: LCSH: Refuse and refuse disposal--Juvenile literature. | Pollution--Juvenile literature.
Classification: LCC TD792 .F59 2017 | DDC 363.72/8--dc23
LC record available at lccn.loc.gov/2016030510

Printed in the United States of America
17/QGT-QGL/1